the Great Dreamer

The Life and Mission of St Francis Xavier

Brendan Comerford SJ

Published by Messenger Publications, 2024

ISBN: 9781788126632

Designed by Brendan McCarthy
Typeset in Adobe Caslon Pro
Printed by Hussar Books

Messenger Publications,
37 Leeson Place, Dublin D02 E5V0
www.messenger.ie

Table of Contents

Preface

The feast of the Jesuit priest and missionary, St Francis Xavier, falls on 3 December. It is usual in the Roman Catholic Church to celebrate a saint's feast on the actual date of his or her death, which is considered to be the date of his or her birth into the fullness of life with God.

The Feast of Francis Xavier 1987 is forever engraved on my memory. At the time I was a student ('scholastic' in Jesuit terms) for the priesthood in Rome. In the Jesuit residence, the Collegio del Gesù, we were some seventy scholastics from thirty-five different countries – the only language we had in common was Italian – in varying degrees of proficiency! On the morning of the Feast of Francis Xavier some of us had four hours of lectures in the Gregorian University – you can imagine that we were somewhat bunched after that. We returned to the Jesuit residence for a community Mass which was to be celebrated by a newly ordained Spanish Jesuit. When it came to the homily this Jesuit went on and on for a full forty-five minutes describing the travels by sea and missionary work of Francis Xavier in the Far East in such minute detail that we were almost all seasick and exhausted. When this young priest told us that Xavier eventually died off the coast of China on 3 December 1552 at the age of forty-six, a Czech scholastic in the congregation voiced the sentiments of the whole community when he said, in deep Slavonic Italian, '*Rendiamo grazie a Dio*' – 'Let us give thanks to God.' When we read the life of Xavier, of his missionary zeal and fervour, perhaps we will have more legitimate reasons to be grateful to God!

I should mention here that the Jesuit student residence in Rome housed the rooms where St Ignatius of Loyola, one of the founders of the Society of Jesus, lived for some sixteen years. Right beside the residence is the magnificent Baroque Church of the Gesù, where the tomb of St Ignatius is to be found at one side altar and, directly opposite, at another side altar, there is a reliquary of St Francis Xavier – one of his arms, in fact. This may seem gruesome to some readers but is basically the product of the devotion of former years. The relic is still greatly reverenced when it is brought around the world, just like the relics of the great Carmelite, St Thérèse of Lisieux.

In the writing of this short biography of Francis Xavier I have relied heavily on the mammoth scholarship of Georg Schurhammer SJ, who wrote a definitive, four-volume, detailed biography of Xavier entitled *Francis Xavier – His Life, His Times,* translated by M. Joseph Costelloe SJ. I am also indebted to four other works: *The Letters and Instructions of Francis* Xavier, translated and introduced by M. Joseph Costelloe SJ; *St Francis Xavier*, by James M. Brodrick SJ; *St. Francis Xavier – The Mystical Progress of the Apostle*, by Xavier Léon-Dufour SJ, translated from the French by Henry Pascual Oiz SJ; and *Unto the Indies – Life of St. Francis Xavier* by Luis M. Bermejo SJ. (Full details of all the works cited can be found in the Select Bibliography, p. 101).

To facilitate the reading of this biography I have deliberately chosen not to have footnotes or endnotes but have inserted any references into the actual text of the narrative. I trust that this will make for easier reading.

Brendan Comerford SJ

Chapter 1

The Early Years

Francisco de Jassu y Azpilicueta was born on 7 April 1506 in the Castle of Xavier, which is located on a hill in the town of Javier (Navarre, Spain), fifty-two kilometres east of Pamplona. It dates back to the tenth century, with various structural additions over the centuries. This medieval stronghold in Spanish Navarre, with its Basque name of 'Xavier', was never of much importance in either war or peace. It ranked very low in the hierarchy of Spanish castles. The name 'Xavier' means nothing more romantic than 'New House', like 'Casanova' in Italian or 'Maison Neuve' in French.

Francis Xavier's parents bore elaborate Basque names ringing with pride of race and place – Don Juan de Jassu y Atonda and Doña María de Azpilcueta y Aznarez de Sada. Don Juan was of farming stock. He attended the University of Bologna where he acquired a doctorate in law. Law was the surest ladder to success in a land as feudalised and litigious as Navarre. Sometime between 1470 and 1480 Don Juan married María, who brought to him as part of her dowry the Castle of Xavier. María claimed descent from a medieval duke reputed, rightly or wrongly, to have been an ancestor of the kings of Navarre.

Francis was the third son of his parents and the youngest in the family. Doña María was forty-two at the time of his birth. There were also Miguel and Juan, who were eleven and nine respectively when Francis was born. Francis had two sisters – his eldest sister, Magdalena, would become a lady-in-waiting to Queen Isabella of

Castile but would soon exchange her court robes for the habit of a Poor Clare nun in Gandía. His sister Anna left the Castle of Xavier to marry when Francis was only six.

The site of the castle provided the only entrance from Upper Aragon to Navarre. It had its own little castle church of Santa María, a kitchen, comfortable living quarters, an armoury, a stable and a farm. Beyond the drawbridge there was a parish house (the *abbadía*) with its garden, small cemetery and church beside it. The church of Santa María de Exavierr had a parish priest and two curates, as well as a sacristan for the church in the castle itself. In his *St Francis Xavier* James Brodrick suggests that these ecclesiastics must have been 'the most obscure ecclesiastics to be found in the four corners of Spain!' (p. 19).

It would appear that Francis was bred in an atmosphere of austere Catholic piety. There was a special devotion to the bitter sufferings of the Lord, as evidenced in the extant old crucifix, the *Santo Cristo*, to be seen in the castle to this day. There was devotion to the Blessed Virgin – the old wooden statue of Our Lady of Exavierr stood on the high altar. St Michael the Archangel was the patron saint of the castle. His name was given to the main tower and to the eldest son, Miguel. There was to be a daily Mass and a solemn High Mass every Sunday and feast day. The Divine Office was always to be said in choir and the *Salve Regina* to be chanted each evening at the sound of the castle bell.

Francis's father, Don Juan, can have had little influence on the boy's development. He spent most of his time in Pamplona, attending to his official duties and striving pathetically to prop up the tottering independence of Navarre (Brodrick, p. 21).

The Political Scene

Here, I need to take a detour for a moment to explain something of the convoluted political situation of Navarre. Again, James Brodrick is of great help here. Navarre, at the time of Francis Xavier's birth, was a united kingdom, though divided geographically by the mighty barrier of the Pyrenees. Four-fifths of Navarre lay in Spain, immediately south of the mountains, and the other fifth in France. The French fifth provided the ruling dynasty, the House of Albert. King Henri d'Albert held court in Pamplona.

When Francis was six, Navarre was forcibly incorporated into the dominions of Ferdinand, King of Aragon. King Henri d'Albert died in exile in 1515. The death of King Ferdinand in 1516 was the signal for an abortive rising in Navarre, which brought on the country the cruel vengeance of Ferdinand's Regent, Cardinal Ximenes. Demolition squads arrived at Xavier. Little was left intact but the living quarters, which the Viceroy of Navarre, the Duke of Nájera, spared out of pity for Doña María and her children. There is absolutely no record of what effect this terrible calamity had on the young Francis.

In 1520, the citizens of Castile staged a rebellion against Emperor Charles V, grandson of the late King Ferdinand. A consequence of this was that Navarre had to be largely emptied of its occupying troops and that gave the Navarrese the chance they had been dreaming of. The King of France, Francis I, a born rival of the emperor, dispatched a large army across the Pyrenees to assist them. Francis's two brothers, Miguel and Juan, sallied forth from the castle to join the French invaders.

The French began the bombardment of Pamplona's citadel in May 1521. One of the defenders, Ignatius Loyola (!) was fighting on the side of the emperor, and, therefore, against Francis's brothers. On Pentecost Sunday, 19 May 1521, a cannonball smashed Ignatius's legs – an event that was to turn around his own life and the lives of many others in the course of history. Eventually, the French were heavily defeated. Miguel and Juan fled to the mountains to launch a sort of guerrilla warfare. Miguel was captured and cast into a dungeon in the Pamplona citadel, but he slipped past the guards dressed as a woman. Three years later, a general pardon was granted and Miguel and Juan returned home to their mother and young brother.

The Francis who greeted his brothers on their return was now eighteen years old and had had himself tonsured as a cleric of the diocese of Pamplona. This gesture committed him to nothing but served to exempt him from whatever military service the emperor might impose.

As regards Francis's education, we can only surmise. Perhaps the three priests were his tutors. Whatever form his education took, he emerged sufficiently equipped with Latin to be able to meet the requirements of the University of Paris.

Chapter 2

Paris

In September 1525, Francis set off over the Pyrenees to study at the University of Paris. There is no evidence that he ever saw his birthplace or his family again. After a ride of about three weeks, Francis saw the walls of Paris. The university was situated in the Latin Quarter of the city and consisted of over fifty colleges. It was a student 'republic', with its own laws, officials and jealously guarded privileges. There were about four thousand students from all over Europe.

Student Life in Paris

It would be helpful for a moment to erase any notion that we have of a university of today. The University of Paris had only four faculties – theology, law, medicine and philosophy. The Faculty of Arts or Philosophy exceeded all the others in size and influence. Some of the students were only ten years old or even younger. There was an introductory course in grammar and rhetoric (the art of persuasive speaking or writing) – in short, logic. This lasted one-and-a-half years. Then there was the three-and-a-half-year course in philosophy, which, in the second year, led to the title of 'bachelor', and, in the last year, to the 'licentiate' and 'master of arts'.

The teachers of philosophy were almost all young students who had just received their master's degree and were called 'regents'. The regents supported themselves financially by their teaching while they themselves were also attending lectures in one of the three higher faculties of law, medicine or theology. In seven years, a student could obtain a doctorate in medicine or canon law. It took twelve to thirteen years to obtain a doctorate in theology.

The College of Sainte-Barbe

Francis enrolled in the College of Sainte-Barbe. The college enjoyed a good deal of prestige owing to the patronage of the King of Portugal and to some distinguished professors. The presence of many Spanish and Portuguese students attracted Francis to Sainte-Barbe.

The students at Sainte-Barbe lived in their own individually rented quarters – they usually lived four to five to a room, and, if possible, under the supervision of one of the regents. There, they slept, studied and kept their most needed books. Latin was spoken both in and out of class. Infractions of the rule were punished with the rod. No one was allowed to leave the college without permission of the principal, Diogo de Gouvea.

The students' daily routine was punishing. The bell for rising rang at four o'clock. A second bell called the students to class at five. At six, there was compulsory Mass for everyone, followed by a very lean breakfast. There followed two hours of classes from eight to ten o'clock. Lunch was served at eleven o'clock, at the beginning of which the lives of the saints were read in the refectory. Classes were held again from three to five. Supper was early, at six, followed by a review of the class matter held during the day. A bell called everyone to chapel at nine, after which came bed and lights out. University life was somewhat different in those distant days!

To compensate for the rigours of life and letters at the university, there were plenty of diversions such as pageants, masquerades, public dances in the streets and sports. Francis took a special delight in the sporting activities, and was accounted as one of the finest high-jumpers on the Île de Vaches.

Many of Francis's fellow students, and even his teacher, were morally corrupt – they climbed over the college wall at night.

Francis often joined his friends on their nights out. His cheerful and amiable disposition had soon won him friends in Paris. He and his friends would make the rounds of the Latin Quarter, visiting taverns and houses of prostitution. The result of these fairly frequent night prowls was that some of the students and masters contracted the so-called 'French disease', syphilis. These nocturnal escapades suited Francis's character but, terrified of contracting syphilis, he was careful not to fall into the way of total profligacy.

Very soon after taking up residence at Sainte-Barbe, Francis found himself sharing a room with a new arrival of peasant stock from Savoy, Pierre Favre, his junior by exactly one week. Between the quiet, simple peasant of the Savoyan Alps and Francis, naturally so different, there soon sprang up a deep bond of friendship.

The first one-and-a-half years of the course, which Favre began with Xavier, were dedicated to logic, which was intended to furnish the students with clear concepts and enable them to set forth their views skilfully, to defend them successfully and to recognise and expose immediately the fallacies of their adversaries. The second half of the second year was devoted to Aristotle. This second year of the course prepared the students for the baccalaureate.

Ignatius Loyola

On 2 February 1528, Ignatius Loyola arrived from Barcelona to study in Paris. He had limped the whole way from Barcelona with a little donkey laden with books. His total fortune was a bill of exchange for twenty-five crowns, given him by a kind working woman of Barcelona, Inés Pascuel. To Xavier's barely concealed disgust, Ignatius was assigned the same room as himself and Favre. Xavier seems to have regarded the new lodger as a joke and was sarcastic about Ignatius's efforts to bring people nearer to God. In later years, Ignatius's secretary, Father Juan de Polanco, wrote that Xavier was not at first much taken with Ignatius – *non ei admodum addictus* (Brodrick, p. 41)

In October 1528, Xavier and Favre had begun their third year of philosophy, which was to prepare them for their examination for the licentiate. Early in 1529, Xavier stood for the usual examination for the baccalaureate. Together with the other candidates he held the festive banquet that was customary at the close of the examination.

Xavier's mother died in July 1529. There is no evidence of any correspondence between Xavier and his brothers in relation to this sad event.

One year later, Favre and Xavier did the much more rigorous examination for the licentiate by successfully defending a variety of scholastic theses before a jury of masters in the Church of Saint-Geneviève. From the official records we know that Xavier stood twenty-second in a class of about seventy students, a good result but not exceptional. Such an examination was not only rigorous and solemn – it was also very expensive. The successful candidate was expected to provide a sumptuous banquet for both teachers and fellow students. The master's degree necessitated an even greater expense. At the conferral ceremony, Xavier's teacher, Juan de la Peña, placed the four-cornered biretta upon Xavier's head, as a visible sign of his new status. From that moment, Xavier was officially known as *Magister Franciscus.* Favre postponed his banquet until later.

Having secured his master's degree, Xavier became a regent, that is, a young lecturer in philosophy. In the autumn of 1530, he signed a contract with the rather obscure Collège de Dormans-Beauvais to teach a full three-and-a-half-year course in philosophy. On 1 October 1530, he began to give lectures on Aristotelian philosophy. Twice a year he was expected to give a festive dinner for his students, and, at this time, he received from them the tuition fees for his lectures. He was expected to be in the study hall and at daily Mass in the college chapel in Dormans-Beauvais. He was given an unfurnished room for himself, a servant (Miguel Landivar) and eventual students! As a regular teacher he had to spend seven hours a day in the classroom. Xavier had continued to reside at Sainte-Barbe and was rapidly sinking into debt. Ignatius Loyola quietly procured students for him.

Ignatius repeatedly helped Xavier in his financial difficulties and also found friends for him who imitated Ignatius's own example. Ignatius advised Xavier to listen to the lectures on theology given by the Dominicans or by the Franciscans. Xavier held fast to his dreams for the future and rarely let slip an opportunity to make fun of his Basque countryman for fleeing the world. Towards the end of 1532, two students, twenty-two-year-old Diego Laynez, a man of Jewish origin, and eighteen-year-old Alfonso Salmeron, came to Paris from the University of Alcalà in Spain, having been attracted there by Ignatius's reputation. Xavier directed his banter at them too. Then came Simon Rodriguez, a young Portuguese, studying at Sainte-Barbe on a scholarship granted by the Portuguese king. After him came the rather eccentric Spaniard, Nicholas Alonso, commonly called Bobadilla, from the small Palencian town of his birth. These students, together with Pierre Favre, began to form a group around Ignatius Loyola.

Xavier had already received the tonsure of a cleric of the diocese of Pamplona and, thanks to his noble origin and his family connections, the priesthood opened up a way to wealth and honours. A benefice as a canon in Pamplona would be a sinecure for him. If he returned home as a doctor, he could be sure of a brilliant career. Xavier commissioned a notary to draw up an authorisation so that he could have his title of nobility officially confirmed by the Royal Council and the Supreme Court of Navarre.

In the spring of 1533 the news reached Xavier his sister, Magdalena, an abbess of the Poor Clares, had died in Gandía on 20 January of that year. Xavier's many expenses in Paris had caused concern at the castle of Xavier and serious thought was given to his recall. When Magdalena learned of this, she had written to her brother, Miguel, urging him, in spite of all the difficulties, to continue to support Xavier in his studies, since she hoped that he would become a great servant of God and a pillar of the Church.

Ignatius had taken his examination for the licentiate on 13 March 1533. For some time Xavier had been looking at Ignatius in a different light. Xavier did not find the decision easy. Very gradually, he succumbed to Ignatius's charm. Ignatius himself was later to confess, in the hearing of his secretary, Juan de Polanco, that Xavier was 'the toughest dough he had ever handled'. Xavier gradually gave up his longings for a reputation in the world and decided that he would become a close follower of Christ.

In June 1533, Pierre Favre had to return to Savoy to his aged father for seven months in order to straighten out the family affairs. Xavier and Ignatius had the room at Sainte-Barbe to themselves. One can only imagine the spiritual conversations between them.

A New Life

A new life had begun for Xavier. The first thing that Ignatius was accustomed to recommend to his disciples was a general confession and a daily examination of conscience, and then weekly confession and Communion. On Sunday mornings, Xavier would go with Ignatius and the other students to the monastery of the Carthusians, where they went to confession and received the Eucharist.

At the beginning of 1534, Pierre Favre returned to Paris. Immediately after his return he made the Spiritual Exercises (thirty-day retreat) under the direction of Ignatius Loyola. Favre was ordained sub-deacon on 28 February 1534 and deacon on 4 April. On 30 May 1534 he was ordained priest. He celebrated his first Mass on 22 July, the Feast of Mary Magdalene.

Ignatius and his companions devoted the hot summer of 1534 to long consultation in order to determine their plans for the future. All had decided to make a pilgrimage to the Holy Land. They would renounce all worldly goods and honours. They decided to postpone their departure from Paris to the Feast of the Conversion of St Paul, 25 January 1537, and to prepare in the meantime for their ordination to the priesthood by completing their theological studies. They further decided to make a pilgrimage to Rome before their departure from Venice in order to obtain papal permission for the pilgrimage to Jerusalem, as was required by the constitution of Pope Clement V (1305–14) at the Council of Vienne in France (1311–12).

After all of the above, they would devote themselves with all zeal to the welfare of both believers and nonbelievers, through work in hospitals, preaching and dispensing the sacraments, and they would not accept any stipends for these spiritual ministries. The vow of poverty would come into effect only after the conclusion of their studies, and they would take with them the necessary funds for the trip to the Holy Land.

On 15 August 1534, Ignatius and his companions went through the city gates of Paris to the hill of Montmartre. They came to a little chapel dedicated to St Dionysius, the first bishop of Paris, who, according to tradition, had suffered martyrdom there. St Thomas à Becket (1118–1170) had prayed there a year before his own martyr's death. Pierre Favre celebrated the Mass and, just before Communion, in the presence of the sacred Host, the companions pronounced vows of poverty, chastity and to go to Jerusalem. They were to repeat this profession of vows at Montmartre for the next three years.

In September 1534, after the conclusion of his three-and-a-half years of teaching philosophy in the College of Dormans-Beauvais, Xavier found the time and leisure to make the Spiritual Exercises under the direction of Ignatius. He withdrew into a solitary house to be alone with God. Ignatius visited him from time to time and gave him the material for his meditations. Xavier attended Mass in the neighbouring church and also received Holy Communion on Sundays and assisted at Vespers.

Xavier gave himself to the Spiritual Exercises with great generosity. He abstained completely from food and drink for four days. As a penance for his vanity in the games on the island of the Seine, where he ranked as one of the best jumpers, he tied his arms, hips and feet so tightly that his limbs swelled up and the thin cord could hardly be seen. This would seem somewhat exaggerated to us today, but we are dealing with earlier times and with Xavier's Basque temperament. The Spiritual Exercises were to become Xavier's map of life. From henceforth, Ignatius was the highly revered and beloved 'father of my soul', his 'only father the love of Christ', through whom God had spoken to Xavier's soul. As Luis M. Bermejo SJ writes: 'Not a scrap of information has been preserved that would permit us to peep into Xavier's inner spiritual experience during this month's retreat. Ignatius's traditional Basque reticence was more than matched by Francis's own' (p. 24).

One of the bonds that now kept the small group of companions together was their common study of theology. Lectures in theology were given at the Dominican and Franciscan monasteries, and at the Sorbonne. The *Summa Theologica* of Thomas Aquinas had been in print since 1512 and was held in the highest regard in Paris.

Plans for the Future

According to their original plan the entire group was to have left Paris for Venice in early 1537, but due to the dangerous political situation (war had broken out between France and Spain) it was decided to bring forward their departure to 15 November 1536. Xavier seems to have started his theological studies some time in 1535. Thus, the entire time he devoted to the study of theology amounted to a maximum of one-and-a-half years. As Bermejo concludes, 'We do not hear that later, when in Italy and before his departure for India that Francis ever supplemented the meagre theological knowledge he had acquired in Paris' (p. 27).

In the meantime, Ignatius had returned to his homeland for health reasons. Before his departure, the companions agreed that they would meet up in Venice on the Feast of the Conversion of St Paul, 25 January 1537. Ignatius carried with him letters from his companions to their Spanish relatives. One of these was a letter from Xavier to his brother, Juan, who was now head of the family and living with his aristocratic wife in wealth and leisure at a manor house called Obanos, a little south of Pamplona. Bermejo tells us that this is the only letter from Xavier to his family that has been preserved for posterity. The letter, dated 25 March 1535, is prompted primarily by Xavier's dire financial straits. It is a courteous but begging letter, without any display of brotherly affection. It opens with the frosty word *Señor.* It is peppered throughout with the expression *V. Merced*, meaning Your Honour or Your Worship. The letter continues, 'If Your Honour wishes to do me the kindness of alleviating my great poverty, you can give to Lord Ignatius, the bearer of this letter, whatever you may wish to send me' (Quoted in Costelloe, *The Letters & Instructions of Francis Xavier*, p. 5).

By 1536, the number of companions had increased with the addition of three excellent students recruited by Pierre Favre. They were Claude Le Jay, Paschase Broët and Jean Codure. Le Jay and Broët had already been ordained. Pierre Favre became the head of the small group after Ignatius's departure. As the companions were making preparations for their departure for Venice in November 1536 an unexpected message came from Pamplona with an official document of the cathedral chapter for Xavier. This informed him that he had been elected to a canonical benefice in the cathedral, and that he should, if he so wished, appear within a fixed time to take the habit of the Canons of St Augustine and begin his year's novitiate. Xavier wrote a letter of thanks to the head of the chapter, declining the offer.

Departure for Venice

On 15 November 1537, the companions left for Venice. Xavier had spent eleven years in Paris. Bermejo gives a detailed and vivid description of the hardships they endured on the journey (pp. 31–33). Owing to the war between Charles V of Spain and

Francis I of France, the companions decided to journey into Italy through Lorraine, Germany and Switzerland. They travelled on foot, each wearing a cassock and the broad-brimmed hat of a Paris student and carrying in a knapsack a change of linen, a bible and a breviary. They used staffs in pilgrim fashion and wore rosaries around their necks as badges of faith and of devotion to the Mother of God. It rained incessantly all the way to Metz, and then, right up to the Italian frontier, they had frost and snow. When held up by marauding soldiers, they stuck to the one answer, given in French or Spanish as the occasion demanded, that they were students from Paris on pilgrimage to a popular shrine near Nancy.

They travelled approximately thirty miles a day on foot and by the time they reached Basle, in Switzerland, winter had already set in. In Basle every trace of Catholic worship had disappeared. The Eucharist was no longer celebrated. The cathedral had been desecrated; the altars had been despoiled of the statues of the saints and the building itself had been converted into a rope factory. The companions reached Venice on 6 January 1537, having been on the road for almost eight weeks. We can only imagine their joy and relief at meeting up with Ignatius again.

Chapter 3

Venice and Rome

When the companions arrived in Venice, they rested for some days, then decided to devote themselves to the service of the sick, to make a pilgrimage to Rome for the Feast of Easter and to obtain permission from the Pope to make a pilgrimage to the Holy Land and to be ordained. Ignatius sent five of them to the hospital near San Giovanni e Paolo in the north of Venice and five to the hospital of the Incurables. Ignatius himself continued his study of theology. Favre, Xavier and Laynez went to the hospital of the Incurables.

After two months of nursing and caring, the companions, with the exception of Ignatius, began their journey to Rome. Ignatius decided to stay in Venice because of the presence of two important men in Rome whom he suspected of being hostile to him – Cardinal Gian Pietro Carafa, the future Pope Paul IV, and Doctor Pedro Ortiz, an emissary of the Emperor Charles V. Ortiz had been critical of Ignatius in Paris.

The companions were without provisions or money, for they now wished to practise poverty and to trust in the providence of God. On their way to Rome, they recited litanies, sang psalms and were in the best of spirits despite the rainy weather.

On the evening of Palm Sunday, 25 March 1537, the companions passed through the Porto del Popolo in Rome. They found free lodgings in the various national hospices. They begged their daily food from door to door. Some of the wealthy members of the Roman Curia took kindly to the companions and provided free food and lodging in San Giacomo degli Spagnoli, near the Piazza Navona.

After the terrible sack of Rome by Spanish and German soldiers in 1527, the city and its environs resembled a desert. Four-fifths of the houses were uninhabited and the churches had been plundered, desecrated or converted into stables. The population had shrunk from 55,000 to 32,000.

The words and way of life of the companions made a fine impression on Dr Pedro Ortiz, who arranged an audience for them with Pope Paul III in Castel Sant'Angelo. The Pope liked to listen to philosophical and theological disputations when he was eating, so the companions stood around his table and disputed with other theologians. The Pope is reported to have said, 'It is a great consolation and joy for me to see such learning united with such modesty. If you need anything from me, I shall gladly grant it to you … but I am afraid that you will not get to the Holy Land' (Schurhammer, Vol. I, p. 336). The Pope gave the companions some financial assistance, as did the cardinals and members of the Curia, especially the Spaniards.

On the way back to Venice, Xavier travelled with Laynez and slept next to him in the hospitals. Many times when Xavier awoke he told Laynez: 'Jesus, how exhausted I am! Do you know what I dreamt? I dreamt that I was carrying an Indian on my back and he was so heavy that I was almost crushed' (Schurhammer, Vol. I, p. 339).

On 10 June 1537, Ignatius, Xavier, Rodrigues, Bobadilla and Codure were ordained priests. Salmerón was still too young and had been ordained a deacon. The ordaining bishop later declared that he had ordained many in the past, but never with such joy and consolation. (Schurhammer, Vol. I, p. 343).

Three Months of Solitude

Because of the threat of war with the Turks, there could be no further thought of making a pilgrimage to the Holy Land in the near future. The companions decided to withdraw into solitude for three months in order to devote themselves entirely to prayer.

They begged from door to door for their daily needs; after the passage of the first forty days, they engaged in some public preaching. They divided themselves into groups of two and three, and it was decided by lot where the various groups would go. Monselice, not far from Venice, fell to Xavier and Salmerón. They walked south for four hours.

Xavier and Salmerón found shelter in a small church dedicated to St George. There were no visitors to disturb the quiet of their retreat and they spent forty days in prayer and meditation. Each week they exchanged roles as superior and subject in order to practise the virtue of obedience. They went to the cathedral every day to assist at Mass. They begged their food daily from door to door. Their greatest mortification was the mosquitos.

The forty days that they devoted to the contemplative life ended during the first week of September and it was now time for the companions to carry out their aim of combining prayer with apostolic labours. They began by preaching in the public squares of Monselice. They would obtain a bench from a neighbouring inn or house, stand upon it, cry out, and invite the people to gather by waving their hats. Some came up to them under the impression that they were jugglers! A good many could hardly understand anything of the preachers' extraordinary mixture of Spanish, French, Italian and Latin, but they were nonetheless impressed by their sincerity and by the fact that they would not take any money.

Two or three weeks had barely passed when Ignatius unexpectedly summoned his companions to Vicenza, towards the end of September. Xavier and Salmerón reached Vicenza at the end of September 1537. Ignatius, Favre and Laynez had set up a house in an abandoned monastery. The place was a haven for mosquitos. The companions came down with fever one after another. Twice a day two of them went into the city to beg for their food from door to door. Three or four of them also preached at times in the public squares.

On 30 September 1537, the feast of St Jerome, Xavier offered his First Mass in the monastery church of San Pietro in Vivarolo.

He always had a great devotion to St Jerome (349?–420). One night, as Xavier was lying awake, it seemed to him that this saint appeared to him and said, 'You will spend the winter in Bologna and you will have to suffer many difficulties there. Some of the others will go to Rome, and some to Padua, Ferrara and Siena.' And so it turned out (Schurhammer, Vol. I, p. 367). Ignatius, Favre and Laynez were to go to Rome. Xavier and Bobadilla went to Bologna.

Bologna

The teachings of Martin Luther had found their way over the Alps, and especially to Bologna, where many German students were to be found. Xavier instructed children, preached to adults, and heard confessions in the Church of Santa Lucia. He soon spent almost the entire day in the confessional. What drew many penitents to Xavier was the high regard they had for his sanctity. While Xavier was staying in Bologna, a young Spanish priest by the name of Juan Jerónimo Doménech stopped there on his way to Rome. He became a friend to Xavier and Bobadilla. Doménech, who later became a Jesuit himself, said that at that time Xavier had spoken mostly of India and of the conversion of the infidels and had shown a great zeal for this and a great longing to go there. (Léon-Defour, *St Francis Xavier,* p. 35).

Bobadilla and Xavier had succeeded in reintroducing a frequent reception of the sacraments in Bologna. They were also effective in their opposition to what they saw as 'heresy' – Lutheranism. On 31 March, a pile of Lutheran books was burned on the Piazza Maggiore.

Rome

Xavier and Bobadilla left Bologna for Rome around the middle of April 1538. They arrived in Rome around Easter ,which fell on 21 April. A palazzo was placed at their disposal by a Messer Quirino

(Schurhammer, Vol. I, p. 408). The companions were provided with extensive faculties (permission to preach and administer sacraments) by Cardinal Gian Pietro Carafa (the future Pope Paul IV) and they began to preach in different churches in Rome. Their sermons created a sensation and drew large crowds, for, as a rule, only monks and friars preached in Rome, and they generally did this only during Lent and Advent.

The Church of San Luigi de' Francesi, frequented by the French colony, became the scene of Xavier's labours, probably because his knowledge of French, after eleven years in Paris, was better than his hit-or-miss Italian.

In June 1538, the companions moved to a house near the Ponte Sisto in the centre of the city, rented for them by their friends. In October, these benefactors obtained another house for them not far from the Capitoline Hill. The house belonged to the Frangipani family. It was thought to be haunted and no one else wanted to live there.

Luis M. Bermejo tells us (p. 41) that soon after the arrival of the companions in Rome dreadful rumours about them began to spread throughout Rome. It was said that these *preti riformati* – 'reformed priests' – as they were called, were in reality nothing but a band of Lutherans who were spreading the dangerous doctrine contained in their esoteric *Spiritual Exercises*. It was claimed that they had been tried for their immoral lives in Spain and France and in other Italian cities, and had come to Rome to start a new order without papal approval. Their ringleader, Ignatius, was the most infamous of all. These rumours were spread by some Spanish members of the Roman Curia and some Capuchins, but chiefly by a certain Miguel Landivar, Xavier's former servant in Paris, who wanted to take revenge on Ignatius because he had been rejected as a companion. In Venice he had been numbered among the companions for a time. He proved himself to be impossible and Ignatius had to let him go. Ignatius demanded an official enquiry and prosecuted Landivar before the Governor of Rome. Landivar was expelled from Rome as a shameful liar and calumniator. A final judgement, dated 18 November 1538, declared the companions to be not only absolutely innocent of the charges brought against them, but priests of the highest probity and orthodoxy.

There followed a very harsh winter and a famine in Rome. The companions went through the streets and brought the homeless to their residence, the Palazzo Frangipani. They begged for the bread, vegetables and wood they needed and kept a large fire burning. After feeding the poor, they instructed them in Christian Doctrine and the most essential prayers and prepared them for the reception of the sacraments, a good confession and Holy Communion, since their ignorance of religious matters was appalling. Alms began to pour in, for the selfless dedication of the 'reformed priests' had made an impression on the Roman population. A secular priest of ample means, Pietro Codazzo, was so impressed that he gave himself over entirely to Ignatius and became the first Italian Jesuit.

In 1538, Diogo de Gouvea, principal of Sainte-Barbe in Paris, drew the attention of King John III of Poprtugal to his former charges, Favre, Xavier, Rodriguez and Ignatius, of whose activities in Italy he had been receiving glowing accounts. Pope Paul III was already sending some of the early companions on missions in Italy. Ignatius and Xavier stayed in Rome. Xavier became Ignatius's secretary since he was constrained at the time by poor health to remain at home. While Xavier was in Rome at Ignatius's side, carrying on the correspondence with his absent companions as secretary of the Society, things were developing that would bring Xavier to the forefront. The intermediary for this was Dom Pedro Mascarenhas, the ambassador of the Portuguese king, at the papal court. John III wanted some Jesuits for the Indies. Pope Paul III decided to send two Jesuits to India as his legates, leaving the choice to Ignatius and his companions. They discussed the issue democratically and, after prolonged prayer, decided to assign the mission to Rodrigues and Bobadilla. Simon Rodrigues rejoiced at the news of this mission. He had always wanted to preach the Gospel in pagan lands.

Dom Pedro Macarenhas had sent his baggage and servants ahead by sea to Lisbon along with Rodrigues and an Italian secular priest, known as Micer Paolo (Paul of Camerino), for he had no family name. He later became a Jesuit and laboured quietly and without show in what would be the College of St Paul in Goa until his death in 1560.

On 14 March 1540, Bobadilla arrived in Rome, but in a wretched state. The cruel Maltese fever afflicted him and the house physician declared that a trip to Portugal in such a condition was unthinkable. Ignatius, who was sick in bed himself, summoned Xavier and said '*Esta es vuestra empresa*' ('This is a task for you.'). To this Xavier replied with readiness '*Pues, sus! Héme aquí*' ('Good enough! I am ready.').

Xavier hastily repaired some old clothes, received the Pope's blessing and said farewell to his friends. He gave his approval to all the Constitutions, Rules and Ordinances that his companions who remained would draw up. He left his sealed vote for Ignatius as Superior-General and, if he should die, then Pierre Favre.

On the Road to Lisbon

On the journey to Lisbon, Xavier made himself the servant of all. When they stopped at an inn, he was the first to take care of the horses and give them fodder. He charmed others with his amiability. The travellers, who included Pedro Mascarenhas, reached Bologna by Easter and continued through Modena and Parma. They travelled through the mountainous country of Guipuzcao, Ignatius's native province in the Basque region of Spain. James Brodrick asks why Xavier did not turn aside to Navarre to say goodbye to those who remained of his family. Perhaps he did and said nothing about it (p. 82)? They stopped off at Loyola, where Xavier presented Ignatius's letters. Xavier says nothing about his visit to Loyola. The party rode all the way across the Castilian plain and on to Lisbon, which they reached at the end of June 1540.

Chapter 4

Lisbon

At the time of Xavier's arrival on 27 June 1540, Lisbon numbered more than 60,000 inhabitants. About a tenth of these were black slaves, both men and women. They were to be found in almost every house, performing all the menial tasks. The city itself was the heart of the vast Portuguese empire, stretching out west to the newly discovered world as far as the Amazon River in Brazil, and east to the distant Spice Islands or Moluccas (present-day Indonesia).

Simon Rodrigues had arrived in Lisbon at the end of April 1540. He tells us that Xavier, on his arrival, was 'appalled and daunted by the heat' (Brodrick, p. 84). Rodrigues and Micer Paolo were living in a house that King John III had rented for them not far from the royal palace. Three or four days after Xavier's arrival, the king summoned him and Rodrigues. The king and queen, Doña Catarina (sister of Charles V of Spain), received them in their private chambers with great kindness. The audience lasted a full hour and the king and queen asked about the companions in detail.

The king asked Rodrigues and Xavier to hear the confessions of the young knights of the court (more than one hundred of them!) every Friday, and also, on other days, of others who were older and were among the leaders of the realm. They also heard the confessions of some of the leading ladies. They introduced the practice of frequent confession and Communion and found the people very well disposed.

Xavier had moved into the house occupied by Rodrigues and Micer Paolo. Despite all the offers of the king, they begged their food daily from door to door. The people simply called them 'the apostles' since they had heard that their Society had been founded by twelve priests in Rome who lived an apostolic life like the disciples of the Lord. It had even been rumoured that they had come dry-shod across the Tagus River and that they had sailed into Lisbon on their outspread mantles, supporting themselves on their staffs! Because of their increasing apostolic labours, the companions finally accepted the food sent by the court and restricted their begging to two days a week.

So many individuals in high positions chose them as their spiritual directors that they did not have time to fulfil all their requests. The king himself spoke to them about the affairs of his soul. Rodrigues and Xavier carried on their activities outside of the royal circle and gave the First Week of the Spiritual Exercises to many of their penitents. Some of the court were striving to prevent their departure for India for it seemed to them that they would gain more spiritual fruit in Lisbon by hearing confessions, engaging in spiritual conversations, giving the Spiritual Exercises, dispensing the sacraments, promoting frequent confession and Communion and preaching than if they were in India. There was a rumour that the king would write to the Pope to ask for his consent to this.

The Inquisition had been introduced into Portugal in 1536 at the insistence of King John. The king's younger brother, the Infante Dom Henrique, Archbishop of Braga, had been appointed Grand Inquisitor. At his bidding, Xavier and Rodrigues went every day to visit prisoners of the Inquisition in order to hear their confessions and to instruct them in the faith. Xavier wrote to Rome on 22 October 1540, 'From the First Week of the Exercises they draw no little fruit' (Schurhammer, Vol. I, p. 644).

On 20 September 1540, the first *auto-da-fé,* or solemn trial of the Portuguese Inquisition was held in the presence of the king, the nobles, prelates and Rodrigues and Xavier. Twenty-three 'heretics' were called to make a retraction of their heretical views. Two of them were burned at the stake. At the explicit request of the Grand Inquisitor, Xavier and Rodrigues stood by the condemned until the last moment. The two were a relapsed French cleric and a Portuguese Jew. The others were sentenced to life imprisonment (Bermejo, p.56).

On 8 October 1540, Rodrigues wrote a letter to Ignatius saying that both he and Xavier were surprised that they had received no mail from Rome for such a long time. In fact, during his nine-month stay in Lisbon, Xavier wrote four letters to Ignatius and received no reply. In the same letter, Rodrigues writes: 'With respect to the Indies, Master Francis and I are somewhat worried that we may be prevented from going. From what we hear the king does not wish it, since he says that we are much needed by his court; we have spoken to him but we were unable to learn anything ... Send us your opinion with regard to this ... (Costelloe, p. 27).

After receiving Rodrigues's letter, Ignatius had gone to Pope Paul III. Since the Pope had designated the two priests for India, it was up to him to decide what should be done. Paul declared that he would leave it up to the king. Ignatius wrote that Rodrigues and Xavier could therefore comply with the desires of the king without scruples about breaking their vow of obedience to the Holy Father. Ignatius added that if the king wished to know his own opinion, it was as follows: Xavier should sail for India but Rodrigues should remain in Portugal in order to reap the harvest there and to attract necessary recruits for the order by the founding of a college in Coimbra and, in this way, provide for the Indies. The king accepted this proposal.

Prior to his departure for the Indies, in a letter of 18 March 1541, Xavier wrote to his companions in Rome, 'When you write to us in the Indies, mention everyone, since it will be but once a year; and write at great length, so that we may keep reading for eight days ...' (Costelloe, p. 39). This typical expression of Xavier's is repeated innumerable times later on. It discloses the very deep attachment of his affectionate temperament to his Jesuit brothers.

So, Rodrigues was to remain in Portugal. Two others were to travel with Xavier: Micer Paolo Camerino and Francis Mansilhas, a Portuguese who was later ordained in Goa. Brodrick writes of the latter, 'he had little or no education and even less capacity to be educated!' (p. 88). There was also a boy named Diego Fernandez, a relative of Rodrigues.

Xavier began his preparations for the voyage to India. When the royal officials offered him their services and asked him to draw up a list of things that he and his companions would need for the voyage, he thanked them for their kindness but said that he had no need of anything except their prayers. When Xavier was urged by a Portuguese nobleman to take at least one servant with him, since he would lose the esteem and authority of the people he was to instruct if they saw him washing his clothes on the ship's deck with the other passengers and cooking his food in the ship's kitchen, Xavier replied: 'Sir, Count, the attempt to procure esteem and authority through the means suggested by Your Lordship has brought the Church of God and its ministers to the state in which they are now in. The way for a man to gain esteem and authority for himself is to wash his own clothes and to take care of his own cooking without thinking about getting help from anyone else, and, at the same time, to labour for the salvation of his neighbour' (Schurhammer, Vol. I, p. 708).

A few days before his departure, Xavier was summoned to an audience with King John III. He was given a papal brief appointing him as nuncio. His powers were considerably restricted. He was to be subject to the local bishop, if there were one, and his faculties amounted to a series of canonical dispensations in marriage, normally reserved to the Pope, and to the possibility of reconciling heretics and schismatics. His authority, however, spread far and wide, 'to all princes and lords of the islands of the Red, Persian and Oceanic Seas and to the provinces and cities on the near and far side of the Cape of Good Hope and the neighbouring lands'. In other words, Xavier was made nuncio of the immense territory that lay between South Africa and Japan (Bermejo, p. 58).

The India fleet for 1541 comprised five very large ships. Their flagship was the *Santiago*, under the command of the newly appointed governor of India, Dom Martim Affonso de Sousa. The *Santiago*, on which Xavier and his companions sailed, was the only royal ship bound for India that year. It held over 700 tons and was carrying a great deal of merchandise. The other four ships belonged to four entrepreneurs. They set sail on 7 April 1541, Xavier's thirty-fifth birthday. Xavier would never see Europe again.

Chapter 5

India

The Voyage

Soon after leaving Lisbon the sea became very rough. Seasickness took its toll of victims. Xavier suffered from it for two months. Nevertheless, the last three days of Holy Week (the Easter Triduum) were celebrated with the same ceremonies as on land. South of the Cape Verde Islands, seven to eight degrees north of the Equator, began the dreaded doldrums, a sea of no winds, a sea where ships could be stuck for up to sixty days. The tropical heat was oppressive. Food became spoiled. Drinking water turned yellow and stank. Scurvy and fever broke out. The *Santiago* soon became a floating hospital. From morning until evening Xavier visited the sick. He begged for his daily food and for whatever he needed for the sick and poor from the captain and the *fidagos* (nobles).

Although Xavier continued to be seasick, he preached on Sundays and feast days. Every evening he gave instructions in the faith on the main deck to the children, cabin boys, slaves and crew. His simple and cheerful manner won the hearts of the hardest sinners and induced them to go to confession. He was called 'the holy father'. The favourite word used by the passengers to describe Xavier was *alegre*, meaning 'cheerful', 'merry', in both Spanish and Portuguese.

Mozambique

At last, after forty days, the Trade Winds began to fill the sails and, at the beginning of June, the *Santiago* crossed the Equator and continued towards the Cape of Good Hope. The ship was tossed about like a nutshell and the air was noticeably cooler. They journeyed on up the East African coast where they saw Moorish settlements near those of the native Africans. At last, they arrived in Mozambique, known as the grave of the Portuguese because of its unhealthy climate. Xavier and his companions stayed in the hospital and tended to the sick.

When the ships from Portugal had docked at Mozambique, bloody, and even fatal, fights and duels were the order of the day; for here, where the men were freed from the supervision of their ships' captains, they were accustomed to avenge the grievances they had experienced during the voyage; and here, just as on the *Santiago*, Xavier exercised the role of peacemaker.

Towards the end of December 1541, Xavier was ill, wracked by fever. His exertions, the long, difficult voyage, the unhealthy climate of Mozambique, and his self-sacrificing care of the sick of the fleet had exhausted his strength. On 1 January 1542, still sick, he wrote his first letter from Mozambique to his brothers in Rome. He concludes the letter, 'I have been bled for the seventh day today and am feeling only fairly well. May God be praised!' In the same letter, Xavier writes of his being occupied in Mozambique hearing confessions, giving Communion and in helping souls at the point of death (Costelloe, p. 41).

Xavier had to spend six months in Mozambique (August 1541 to February 1542) waiting for the April monsoon to waft them to their destination across the Indian Ocean and the Arabian Sea (Bermejo, p. 70). Many of the sick had to be left behind; Micer Paolo and Francis Mansilhas, at the request of the governor, Dom Martim Affonso de Sousa, remained in Mozambique to care for them. Xavier, however, had to accompany the governor. Affonso's health had been worn down by the damp, feverish air and he wanted to have Xavier at his side during the voyage in order to be able to confess to him in case of need.

Goa

At the end of February 1542 the *Coulam* sailed from Mozambique. It was a new vessel, a galleon, easy to manoeuvre, and built for combat and swift progress. Xavier resumed his earlier apostolate on the *Coulam*. He reserved his cabin for the sick, taking his own rest as a rule on the coiled ropes of the ship, using the anchor for a pillow!

On 6 May 1542, the *Coulam* arrived in Goa, the capital of Portuguese India. It had taken Xavier a year and twenty-nine days to reach India. As papal nuncio a residence was put at his disposal. Though he was received with the greatest kindness, he refused everything that was offered him. He went to the royal hospital and, as a poor religious, asked for a place to stay. A poor little cottage next to the main building was given him as a residence.

Xavier paid his first visit to the local bishop, Fray Juan de Albuquerque, a Franciscan friar. Goa had become a diocese only eight years before Xavier's arrival. The bishop's diocese was the largest in Christendom – it embraced all of the lands east of the Cape of Good Hope, even though it had only thirteen parishes. Xavier informed the bishop that Pope Paul III and King John III had sent him to India to help the Portuguese, to instruct the new converts, and to labour for the conversion of the 'infidels'.

Living in the hospital, Xavier spread out his mat at night near the bed of the person most seriously ill and most in need of help so that he might always be at hand in case of emergency. His daily routine was simple. In the morning he performed his spiritual exercises at an early hour and celebrated Mass in the hospital chapel. He then gave his attention to the sick, hearing their confessions and bringing them Holy Communion. After midday, he made it his custom to go around the city's three prisons, dirty, ill-smelling places, with no drain from the sewer to the outside. They were also overcrowded. Xavier taught the prisoners how to make a good general confession.

Xavier was also concerned about the lepers. He went to the leprosarium early on Sunday mornings and celebrated Mass for them. They made their confessions to him and received Holy Communion from his hand. Xavier said of the lepers: 'They have become my very good and devoted friends' (Schurhammer, Vol. I, p. 211).

A great hardship for the Portuguese in India was the absence of European women. Portuguese women were strictly forbidden to sail there. The men were to marry native women of light complexion and better social standing, especially Mohammedan women. The women were baptised and received a Christian name before their marriage. They lived very secluded lives and were hardly or not at all instructed in their new faith, with the consequence that they often relapsed into their former superstitious practices (Bermejo, p. 73). Bishop Albuquerque had ordered the priests to teach them their prayers in church after the noon meal.

There was no lack of priests. In Goa and its environs there were about a hundred, including the Franciscans. The clergy, however, left much to be desired. Most lacked the learning required for their vocation. They did not even have an adequate knowledge of Latin, let alone a sound theological training. Many lived openly with concubines and were more concerned with their trade than with the spiritual welfare of their flocks, for they had come to the Indies with the sole intention of returning to Portugal as rich men. Preaching was hardly practised at all. Religious instruction had fallen into disuse.

In the evenings, when it was cooler, Xavier went with a little bell through the streets and squares of Goa and cried out: 'Faithful Christians, friends of Jesus Christ, send your sons and daughters and your slaves, both men and women, to learn about the faith, for the love of God!' (Schurhammer, Vol. II, p. 220). He led them to the church of Nossa Senhora de Rosario. More than three hundred would frequently be brought together for instruction. Xavier would sing the lesson in order to impress it more deeply upon the minds of his hearers. Two boys, and then all the rest together, had to repeat his words. This was followed by the Creed, the Our Father, the Hail Mary and other parts of the catechism, such as the Ten Commandments, the Confiteor, the prayers before and after meals. There was much more.

After an-hour-and-half or two hours Xavier concluded the lesson with a prayer to the Mother of God, three Hail Marys or the Salve Regina (Schurhammer, Vol. II, p. 220).

At night, Xavier went again with his little bell through the streets of Goa and invited the residents to pray for the souls in purgatory and for those living in a state of mortal sin and who did not wish to be converted.

Xavier's main means of winning over sinners was his own personal dealings with them. His cheerful manner seems to have been irresistible. He was generally a welcome guest in the houses of the Portuguese. He learned from friends if a master was keeping slaves as concubines. He would seek out the man and, with a cheerful expression, would invite himself to dinner! His conversation was pleasant. He praised everything. At the end of the meal he also wanted to see the cook. The slave was called. He praised her cooking, thanked her for a good reception, told her she should become a saint (!) and took his leave of his host. There was no reference to the latter's sinful life or exhortation to repentance, but Xavier's visit was often sufficient to bring the sinner to his senses and move him to give up his illicit relations.

In confession, Xavier encouraged the penitent. He spoke of the great mercy of God. As a penance he liked to give a fixed time for practising 'The First Method of Prayer' taught by Ignatius Loyola in the *Spiritual Exercises* [238–248]. Morning and evening they should meditate upon the Ten Commandments, the Seven Deadly Sins (pride, anger, envy, lust, gluttony, avarice and sloth). Just in passing, it is interesting to mention that the only book, besides his breviary and a species of catechism that Xavier is known to have brought with him (which still exists), is a small thick volume, published in Cologne in 1531, containing the work of Eusebius of

Caesarea (c.265–c.340), John Cassian (c.360–435) and other theological writers (Brodrick, p. 96). It was compiled by Marcus Marulus (1452–1524), a Croatian poet and humanist, and in this book Xavier found examples for his preaching and instructions. He preferred to study the living books, the people with whom he associated.

On this first occasion, Xavier spent less than five months in Goa. In a series of long letters to Ignatius and to his companions (20 September 1542), Xavier wrote of Goa being a land 'so subject to the sins of idolatry, and so difficult to dwell in because of the great heat'. He begs his brothers in Rome 'to write to me at length about all of the Society! Since I do not expect to see you face to face again in this life, may it be at least through mirrors, that is, through your letters.' He signs off as 'Your useless brother in Christ' (Costelloe, p. 51). This statement reveals something of his humility. Writing to Ignatius Loyola on the same date, he signs off as 'Your son in Christ' (Costelloe, p. 59).

Luis M. Bermejo tells us (pp. 76–77) that apart from the cathedral and the nearby convent of the Franciscans, the hub of Catholic Goa was what would later be referred to indiscriminately as the 'Confraternity of the Holy Faith', or St Paul's College, which was destined to play an increasingly important role in the history of the Society of Jesus in Goa. It had started at the initiative of the Vicar-General of the diocese, Miguel Vaz, and a nobleman, Cosme Anes, both of them being enthusiastically supported from the start by Mestre Diogo Barba, a secular priest.

The above-mentioned had envisioned a college where Indian boys who, after their baptism, showed an inclination for the clerical state, would be trained with a view to becoming missionaries among their own countrymen. In other words, St Paul's would become the first seminary for the clergy set up in India. The number of students should be limited to thirty, and they should all be at least thirteen years old, to ensure that they did not forget their mother tongue. Eventually, they would become parish priests under the bishop of Goa. The Governor of India, Dom Martim de Sousa, supplied funds.

On 20 September 1542, the administration of St Paul's, initially entrusted to the Franciscans, was offered now to the Jesuits – of whom at this stage there was only one in the whole of India – Xavier himself! All he could do was write to Ignatius and ask for more Jesuits. He did. In a letter to Ignatius (20 September 1542), Xavier ask that Ignatius would send a Jesuit who would be occupied solely with the teaching of Latin, which would keep him very busy.

Cape Comorin and the Fishery Coast

The intention of the Governor, Martin de Sousa, was that Goa would be no more than a temporary stop for Xavier. At the end of September 1542, Xavier set out for Cape Comorin and the Fishery Coast. Cape Comorin is situated at the southernmost point of sub-continental India. The distance from Goa is about 600 miles which, with favourable winds, could be covered in ten to twelve days. Today, Cape Comorin is in the state of Tamil Nada and is called Kanyakunari (meaning 'Virgin Princess'). The Paravas ('pearl-fishers') are a Tamil maritime community living mainly in the state of Tamil Nada. The Fishery Coast spreads from Cape Comorin to its chief town, Tuticorin, about sixty miles away. Tuticorin (Thoothukudi today) is an important port in the Bay of Bengal. Xavier spent nearly two years of the ten remaining to him in this world, moving back and forth over its desolate sands.

The Parava people came to greet the newcomers, especially the white Father, the *swami* (an ascetic or religious teacher). There were three Parava seminarians from Tuticorin with Xavier – the deacons Gaspar and Manuel and the third in minor orders. They had been sent to St Paul's in Goa for education in the hope that they might return as priests. Xavier had brought them with him to serve as interpreters. Six years earlier, like the inhabitants of the other Parava villages, they had been baptised and had received a Portuguese first and last name. However, there were no churches in their villages, no Portuguese, no priests, no one to teach the people Christian doctrine. They only knew that they were Christian; they were ignorant of what they should believe since they did not understand Portuguese.

Mass baptisms had taken place in Cape Comorin in early 1536, six years before Xavier landed in Goa. Only the bare sacrament had been administered, without the slightest instruction in the faith, for none of the Portuguese knew Tamil. In 1537, during the so-called Great Fishery, further baptisms took place among the Paravas in the Tuticorin area. When Xavier arrived, a single secular priest was the pastor of all the villages. He seems to have remained in Tuticorin without teaching Christian doctrine or visiting the other villages. In a letter to Ignatius from Tuticorin on 28 October 1542, Xavier says: 'Because the Christians of these villages have no one to instruct them in the faith, they can say nothing more about it than that they are Christians' (Costelloe, p. 61).

Nevertheless, the Paravas brought to Xavier the children who had been born since the last mass baptisms of 1536 and 1537. The Parava children left Xavier no time to rest for saying his Breviary, for eating or sleeping. Xavier taught them their prayers with the help of the three seminarians who had some knowledge of Portuguese.

Tuticorin had a mixed population. A good many pagans lived there among the Christian Paravas and Xavier, for the first time, came into close contact with the pagan beliefs and practices of India. There was a great Hindu temple in Tuticorin. Here, Xavier and the three seminarians encountered Hinduism. As Brodrick tells us (p. 148), Xavier had woefully inadequate views about Indian religion and civilisation. He encountered the high-caste Brahmans – worshippers of Shiva and Vishnu. There were numerous images of the gods in the temples. The Brahmans were the priests of the temples and lived off their revenues. The religion of the pagans was, especially for the common people, a religion of fear.

The whole world was full of evil spirits who had to be pacified with sacrificial offerings. When the Brahmans lacked provisions, they threatened the people with the wrath of the gods in order to obtain what they needed. When a man died, his body was burned and his widow had to follow him into the next world. If a widow refused to allow herself to be burned, she was repudiated by her relatives and condemned to a life of shame.

The priestly caste of the Brahmans proved to be unapproachable. They were the main support of idolatry and their influence on the people was extensive. They were able to relate some fables about their temples and gods, and since they and their wives and children lived off the sacrificial offerings brought to them, they made the ignorant people believe that the gods desired alms and food; they threatened them, if they neglected to bring offerings, with the wrath and vengeance of the gods, who would kill them or send sickness and demons into their homes. When Xavier spoke to the Brahmans in person, they admitted that they deceived the people and composed these tales because the stone idols were their only source of income. They sent gifts to Xavier so that he would not betray their secret. Xavier refused these gifts and told them in no uncertain terms what he thought of them; and he explained the frauds of the priests to the poor. Many thus lost their fear and reverence for the devils and became Christians.

The Paravas had to be instructed in Tamil and this is where the three seminarians, with their partial knowledge of Portuguese became somewhat useful. Xavier could not think of learning the Tamil alphabet. 'It is a mere legend that God endowed Xavier with the miraculous "gift of tongues"' (Brodrick, p. 132). He went through the village with his bell and gathered together all the men and boys he could. For a whole month he continued this instruction, and his hearers had to repeat what they had learned to their parents and other members of the household and to their neighbours.

Bermejo tells us (pp. 88–89) that at the beginning of March every year the annual event of the Great Fishery took place south of the island of Mannar near the south-eastern tip of India, right opposite the coast of Ceylon. As many as fifty thousand came together: vessel owners, divers, sailors, traders, merchants from all parts of India. The low-caste Paravas dived naked, with no other equipment than a net for the oysters and a knife for the sharks. The mussels were to be found at a depth of 5–12 fathoms (about 9–21 metres). The immersion lasted no more than one-and-a-half-minutes. Except for shorts periods of rest, the divers continued their difficult and dangerous work until noon. Many bled from the ears, mouth and nose when they held their breath too long. Many lost consciousness and drowned when they ran out of breath. Some were eaten by sharks. Around noon, after five or six hours of toil, the divers were exhausted. Owing to the necessity of holding their breath for a minute or more on the ocean bed, these unfortunates often acquired an occupational disease of the lungs from which they died young.

After leaving the mussels to dry on the beach for a few days, they were then opened and the pearls extracted. Many of the shells were empty but others were a veritable treasure trove, each containing four to eight shiny pearls. A percentage of the revenue on pearls went to Goa and Lisbon and that seemed to be all that Lisbon and Goa cared about.

Twenty to thirty days after its inception, the pearl fishing came to a close. Xavier then went through the Parava villages. He stayed in each village for a number of days to instruct the people with the help of his interpreters. Once a week he gathered the adults together, the women on Saturday and the men on Sunday, for two hours. He had the Christian truths and prayers repeated and, with the help of his interpreters, Xavier explained them. He relentlessly attacked idolatry. One day he learned that idols had been worshipped in the cottage of a Christian. He ordered the cottage to be burned down as an example to others. He had those guilty of adultery with married women publicly flogged and imprisoned. He also acted strongly against drunkenness.

Among the people he was called the *Periya Padre* ('Great Father' or 'Holy Father)' (Schurhammer, Vol. II, p. 338). He ate very little and spent much of the night in prayer. He frequently slept on the bare ground and if friends or admirers sent him food, he gave it to the poor without tasting it. He adapted his diet to that of the poor fishers. His usual food was rice. He seldom ate meat, and only when he was invited out.

As we have seen, at the time of his arrival, the Paravas had no churches outside of Tuticorn. At first, Xavier would celebrate Mass and give instructions in the shade of a tree. But soon, at his insistence, the villagers would erect a temporary chapel of palm leaves, a *ramada*, as he called it (coming from *rama*, the Spanish for branch), or a more substantial clay chapel with a palm-leaf roof. Each village had a patron for its church. Xavier also had *cruzados* erected – plain, large wooden crosses with two cross arms but no image of Christ. These were painted black and fixed into a whitewashed stone base as a sign of the victory of the Christian faith.

When Xavier had finished his visit to a village, he set out on his way again. Never did he spend an entire month, or even twenty days, in the same place. He had a reputation of being a wonder-worker. From all sides he was summoned to visit the sick and pray over them.

Back to Goa

For more than a year, Xavier remained completely alone at his post and, in late 1543, he made his way back to Goa, 800 miles away, taking with him a few promising Paravan boys for education at the College of St Paul. Thanks to the beneficent care of Dom Martim de Sousa, the activity of Cosme Anes and the secular priest, Mestre Diogo, the college had prospered. The revenues came primarily from the riches of the pagan temples of Goa that had been destroyed in 1541. The college received funds in abundance. Many of the students were learning Latin, while others were learning how to read and write. They were all children of pagan parents and spoke different languages.

On his arrival at St Paul's in mid-November 1543, Xavier was given the mail that had been sent to him from Europe: letters from Rome, dated 13 January 1542, from Ignatius and his companions, which gave him much consolation, and two letters from Simon Rodrigues, from Portugal, written at the beginning of 1542 and 1543. It was the first letter Xavier had received from Ignatius since they parted on 4 March,1540, three-and-a-half years earlier. From March 1540 (the time of his departure from Rome) right up to October 1549 (his appointment as Provincial), Xavier had received only three letters from Ignatius. It is presumed that some letters were lost in transit.

Xavier's first visit on his return to Goa was to the bishop. From Rome Ignatius had sent to Pierre Favre, Simon Rodrigues and Xavier the text of the vow formula for solemn vows which Ignatius and the other companions had used in St Paul's Outside the Walls in Rome in March 1541. Xavier placed the profession of his vows in the hands of his friend, the bishop, and from then on he carried a copy of the vow formula in a copper reliquary about his neck, with the signatures of his beloved spiritual father, Ignatius, and of his first companions, which he had cut from their letters.

Return to the Fishery Coast

Shortly before Christmas 1543, Xavier returned to the Fishery Coast. He took with him four helpers: two Tamil secular priests, Francis Mansilhas, who was not yet ordained, and João de Artiaga, a Spanish layman. Mansilhas and Xavier worked in separate areas of the Fishery Coast. As many as twenty-four letters from Xavier to Mansilhas are extant. Almost the entire correspondence is full of imperatives. In almost every letter Xavier is ordering Mansilhas around. Brodrick tells us (p.165) that it is to the everlasting credit of Mansilhas that he treasured these scraps of correspondence and, when dying, long after the death of Xavier, bequeathed the collection to the Jesuits in Cochin. The originals perished when the Dutch besieged Cochin and destroyed the Jesuit college there in 1663, but many copies had been made and sent to Europe long before that.

This correspondence with Mansilhas spans the ten months from February to December 1544. (Costelloe, pp. 74–107). Brodrick's harsh judgement on Xavier's letters to Mansilhas may be justified: 'Of what trifles they are composed, and how abominably repetitive! There is hardly a grace of style or a profundity of observation in them from beginning to end'(p.188).

Cochin

January 1544 sees Xavier in Cochin (modern-day Kochi, a major sea port on the Malabar Coast of the Arabian Sea in West-Central Kerala State). Xavier made this journey from Cochin to Goa in either direction thirteen times. In a letter to his companions in Rome, from Cochin, dated 15 January 1544, Xavier writes of the young Christian boys who reproach their fathers and mothers when they see them worshipping idols, and they denounce them by coming to Xavier to tell him about it. Xavier mentions how he went with the boys to the place where the idols had been erected; 'the boys take the idols and smash them to bits. They then spit on them and trample them under their feet. These idols were horses and cows of clay, and men of stone, and figures of snakes of stone, peacocks and jackdaws …'(Costelloe, p. 66).

It is in this same letter of 15 January 1544 that Xavier famously writes to his companions in Rome:

> I could never come to an end in describing to you the fruit that is being gained by baptizing new born children and teaching those who are old enough to learn … Many times I am seized with the thought of going to the schools in your lands and crying out there, like a

> man who has lost his mind, and especially at the University of Paris, telling those in the Sorbonne who have greater regard for learning than desire to prepare themselves to produce fruit from it: 'How many souls fail to go to glory and go instead to hell through their neglect!' There is such a multitude of those who are being converted to the faith of Christ in this land where I am that it frequently happens that my arms become exhausted from baptizing and I can no longer speak from having recited the Creed and the Commandments in their language, in which I explain to them what it is to be a Christian, what paradise is, what hell is, telling them what kind of people they are who go to the former and that kind to the latter … There are days when I baptize a whole village, and, on the coast, where I am now there are thirty Christian villages. (Costelloe, pp. 67–68)

Xavier's letters in Spanish or Portuguese caused a real sensation in Europe. They were copied again and again and translated into several languages. Unbeknownst to him, Xavier was considered a real hero. It was the letter he wrote from Cochin on 15 January 1544 (quoted above) that caused the greatest excitement.

Self-disclosure did not come easily to Xavier (Bermejo, pp. 91–93). Moments of transparency when he reveals something of himself to others are few and far between. Sincere effusions of brotherly or filial love span the whole of Xavier's stay in the East and, if anything, they seem to grow even more intense towards the end, at least in regard to Ignatius. For Xavier the Society is 'a Society of love': 'If I should ever forget the Society of the name of Jesus may my right hand be forgotten … The debt which I owe to this holy Society … I am saying this in order to avoid the sin of ingratitude' (Bermejo, p. 93).

At this time there were only three Jesuits in India – Micer Paolo was at St Paul's College in Goa and Masilhas and Xavier were labouring in different parts of the Fishery Coast. I agree with

Bermejo when he writes (p. 97) that temperamentally Xavier was a bit of a paradox. On the one hand, he showed himself to be always outgoing and sociable, kind and jovial, enjoying the company of other people. Yet, on the other hand, his life in the East was often marked by an unusual loneliness, not only because loneliness was thrust upon him, but also because he seems to have deliberately sought it.

On 27 January 1545, Xavier wrote three letters from Cochin to Ignatius, to Simon Rodrigues and to the Roman Jesuits in general (Costelloe, pp. 113–23). The first two letters were largely appeals for more labourers in the huge Indian vineyard: 'Let all the unwanted ones come,' he wrote to Ignatius, 'the men with no talent for hearing confessions or preaching or other ministries of the Society, provided only that they be strong of body and spiritual of soul ... In these heathen places the only education necessary is to be able to teach the prayers and go about baptizing little ones who now die in great numbers without the Sacrament because we cannot be everywhere at once to succour them.' William Brodrick tells us that Xavier entirely changed this mistaken view of the qualities of mind necessary in missionaries later on, as a result of wider experience (p. 205).

In his letter to Rodrigues, Xavier appeals: 'Send many to India, for they will greatly extend the boundaries of our Holy Mother, the Church' (Costelloe, p. 122). After he had received this letter, Rodrigues wished to send ten priests and five brothers to India. Nine of the Society sailed there in 1546.

The third letter of 27 January 1545 gives us a clear picture of Xavier's pastoral method. This letter enthralled not only the Roman Jesuits, but also the wider circles of Catholic Europe:

> ... In a single month I baptized more than 10,000 men, women and children. My method, on arriving in a heathen village, was to assemble the men and boys apart, and to begin by teaching them to make the Sign of the Cross three times as a confession of faith in Father, Son

> and Holy Spirit … I then recited in loud voice … the Creed, the Commandments, the Our Father, the Hail Mary, and the Salve Regina. Two years ago, I copied out those prayers and formulae in the Tamil language which is spoken here and know them by heart … Thereupon, I baptized each one, and handed them his new Christian name written on a slip of paper … The baptisms over, I told the new Christians to demolish the shrines of the idols, and saw to it that they crushed the images into dust. (Costelloe, p. 117)

The letter to the Roman Jesuits telling of the Travancore (most of the south of modern-day Kerala) conversions was meant for general consumption, and was therefore copied by assiduous pens in Portugal before being sent on its way over the Pyrenees. When King John was shown the letter, he said that nothing else in the world could have given him so much satisfaction and directed that the marvellous news was to be proclaimed in all the pulpits of the land. The rector of the Jesuit College in Coimbra wrote to Pierre Favre of the soul-stirring effect the letter had on his young men: 'I think I would have little difficulty in transferring the whole of the college to India' (Brodrick, p. 216). Favre became one of the apostles of the letter, spreading it far and wide in Spain and beyond.

Bermejo rightly asks (p. 101) if the instruction that lasted a little more than an hour or was given through a mechanically memorised sermon was deemed sufficient. The new Christian life of both the Paravas on the Fishery Coast and the Macuas of Travancore was strictly reduced to the baptism they had received. Xavier never learned enough Tamil to hear confessions. The Christianity of the Paravas and the Macuas hung by a thread. After receiving baptism, the 'converts' were left to themselves, without priests and, therefore, without sacraments. It was little wonder that some of them relapsed into their former superstitious practices.

Around this time two Italian Jesuits, Antonio Criminali and Nicolò Lancilotto, arrived in India. Both of them were highly appreciated by Xavier and both were destined to become local superiors. Criminali became the first in a series of Jesuit martyrs. Bermejo tells us (p. 102) that both these men wrote to Ignatius separately, and, in their very first letter, they strongly disagreed with the method of hasty baptism used by Xavier not only in the south, but even in Goa. Criminali wrote that is was 'a burden on his conscience'. Lancilotto later demanded three or four months of instruction before baptism. For six or seven years Ignatius had been hearing complaints from Lancilotto and Criminali about hasty baptisms. Finally, in early 1552, Ignatius wrote to Lancilotto through his secretary, Juan de Polanco: 'Regarding the custom of refusing baptism unless the necessary catechetical instruction has preceded, it seems to be very reasonable' (Bermejo, p. 104).

Bermejo explains to us (p. 104), correctly, I think, that the reason that impelled Xavier on such a mistaken course of action was his wrong theology of salvation of the unbaptised. Subjectively, he acted always in good faith, but objectively, he was grossly mistaken.

It is Thomas Aquinas himself who condemns Xavier: 'If children are to be baptized, the baptism should not be postponed ... But with regard to adults, baptism is not given immediately after their conversion; it should rather be postponed for some time ... so that they may be instructed in matters of faith.' Apparently Xavier had forgotten or had never heard that, according to Thomas, 'it is possible to attain eternal salvation without the actual reception of baptism, because of the baptism of desire' [*Summa* III, q.68. a.3]. Xavier's hurried theology in Paris produced hurried baptisms in India (Bermejo, p. 105).

Lancilotto was the first to point out to Ignatius in 1545 that Xavier's frequent absences were doing more harm than good. Already he complains to Rome that it is 'as if Francis were in Constantinople and we in Rome ... Master Francis could provide things from where he is as if he were in Rome; he knows little about the College [St Paul's, Goa]'. Again, in 1550, Lancilotto wrote, 'Master Francis goes very far from the rest of us, and he cannot direct and take care of things here …' (Costelloe, pp. 166, 324).

Writing to Ignatius, Xavier again speaks of the quality of the men to be sent to India: 'In these pagan lands there is no need for learning beyond what is required for the teaching of prayers, the visiting of villages and the baptism of new born infants … You should, therefore, send those who are not for the Society, but who should be able to go from village to village, baptizing and teaching … The apostolate among the Japanese and Chinese certainly requires learning, but in India we can do with second-class men with no learning worth the name' (Bermejo, p. 107).

Nicolò Lanclotto, from the very beginning, emphasised that learning was needed in India: 'I cannot exaggerate the absolute need of learned and virtuous men for these regions … The men you should send here should be outstanding in learning … Those who say that the men of the Society who come here need not be learned, don't know what they are talking about!' (Bermejo, p. 107; Costelloe, p. 325).

Back on the Fishery Coast, on 7 April 1545, Xavier wrote his last letter to Francisco Manshilas, who had meanwhile been ordained a priest in Goa: 'Constantly keep moving from village to village.' Many years after his death Xavier was to earn the name *El Divino Impaciente* ('The Inspired Hustler') – always restless, always on the move, unwilling to stay in one place (Bermejo, p. 109).

Mansilhas, Xavier's only Jesuit companion in southern India, had been ordained a priest in Goa in early 1545. Several weeks later, he is back on the Fishery Coast but without a word of congratulations in the letter from Xavier (Costelloe, pp. 123–26).

San Thomé

In April 1545, Xavier reached San Thomé (modern Mylapore-Madras). It had a colony of about 500 Portuguese soldiers and merchants. For centuries, San Thomé had been linked with St Thomas the apostle. Xavier was in the habit of wearing around his neck a small reliquary containing a small bone of the saint.

Xavier landed in San Thomé with a doubt as to whether God was calling him to the Macassar Islands (modern Sulawesi in Indonesia). Christian converts had recently been made there. The driving force seems to have been both to look after the existing Christians and to make new ones – consolidation and expansion. During the nearly four months he stayed in San Tomé, Xavier struck up a friendship with his host, the vicar, Gasper Coelho. Not only did they become fast friends, but Xavier took him also for his confessor. According to a later testimony of Coelho himself, sometimes Xavier came for daily confession.

On 8 May 1545, Xavier wrote to Micer Paolo in Goa: 'I deemed it my duty to engage myself in asking God our Lord to grant me to feel within my soul his most holy will … With great interior consolation I have felt and have come to know that it is his will that I go to the regions of Malacca (south-western Malaysia) … God has granted me, with great satisfaction to my soul and spiritual consolation that favour of making me feel … that it is his will that I go to the regions of Macassar' (Costelloe, *Letters*, p. 128).

Chapter 6

Indonesia: Malays and Malacca

Malacca

In September 1545, Xavier's opportunity to sail for Malacca arrived. He travelled with João Eiró, a Portuguese merchant. They were a month on the high seas, covering the 1,700 miles that lay between San Thomé and Malacca. Malacca was one of the world's centres of trade, a seething, sweltering place, not much more than a degree above the Equator.

When he arrived in Malacca, Xavier took up residence with Eiró in the royal hospital, where he found shelter in a cottage near the sea. The Portuguese presence in Malacca was slight: there were sixty to seventy *casados* (married men) and around 200 soldiers to garrison the fortress. The native population was in the region of 20,000, practically all of whom were pagans or Moors. The city was famous for its moral degradation. Male and female slaves of all colours were to be found everywhere.

The ignorance of the people was great. Preaching was neglected, and the teaching of Christian doctrine had lapsed completely into oblivion. Many of the 'New Christians' who had come from Portugal lived openly as Jews or Muslims. 'New Christians' were descendants of Jews or Muslims who had been baptised in Portugal and had abandoned the faith to which they may, or may not, have been truly converted in India. Xavier wrote from Malacca to King John advocating the establishment of the Inquisition at Goa. The original letter is not extant but Xavier makes reference to it when writing again to the king from Amboina on 16 May 1546

(Brodrick, p. 240; Costelloe, p. 149). The Inquisition was finally introduced in India in 1560.

While in Malacca, Xavier took care of the physical and spiritual needs of the sick. He begged for the poor from door to door. He also visited the soldiers of the garrison and, because of his cheerful manner, he was readily received by them. Through his affability he became all to all, and he frequently established peace between the soldiers and the citizens.

In his Sunday morning sermons, Xavier spoke out strongly against the immoral lives of so many – their usury, idolatry, lawsuits, sins of injustice and their other vices. He threatened his listeners with the divine punishments that would come upon the city if they did not mend their ways. Great numbers came to confession as a result!

The worst sinners, those who gave the most scandal by their way of life, did not come to confession. Xavier sought to win their confidence. He invited himself to dine with one and then another. One day he did this with a rich and prominent man who was living with a concubine. When the host and his guest had sat down to eat, Xavier declared that he would not eat without the lady of the house. His host could do nothing but call her and all three dined together. During the course of his conversation Xavier persuaded his host to marry his partner, which he did at once!

It was Xavier's holy life more than anything else that gave him such power over the hearts of others. The Portuguese and even the pagans and Moors called him 'holy father'. He lived on alms as a poor man of Christ and not like the priests who were greedily engaged in trade. Xavier's radiant cheerfulness attracted the hearts of many.

The end of the year was the time when the ships from China were accustomed to return to Malacca. Xavier secured much information about that mysterious land from Portuguese merchants who had returned from there.

Xavier had been able to do much good in the three-and-a half-months of his stay in Malacca. He had baptised many of the pagans and had reconciled many of the Portuguese with God. However, many of the inhabitants of Malacca had refused to give up their vices. Xavier shook the dust from his shoes and said that God was keeping him from taking the dust of such a wicked city as Malacca with him so that he would not contaminate others with it! (Schurhammer, Vol. III, p. 50).

The time had now come for Xavier to depart for the Macassar Islands. For Xavier, Malacca was merely a stage on his route to Macassar and further east. He sailed from Malacca on New Year's Day 1546. The voyage of at least 1,740 nautical miles took one-and-a-half months. The route lay through South China, Java, Flores and the Banda Sea (Brodrick, p. 247). In the course of his subsequent travels, Xavier would come back to Malacca four more times.

Amboina

Because the news from the Macassar Islands was not promising, Xavier decided to sail for Amboina (today, Ambon Island, one of the Moluccas). It was Xavier's first contact with what is now Indonesia. He was accompanied by his faithful friend, John Eiró (the Portuguese sailor turned disciple). They reached Amboina on 14 February 1546.

Amboina was about 120 miles in circumference, with a total of seven villages. The Christians in the communities spread along the coast numbered about 8,000. After their baptism, they had been looked after by a single priest, but when he died after a few years they became a flock without a shepherd. Xavier had to begin almost from scratch.

Manuel, the small son of the village chief of Hatiwi, was Xavier's companion on his visit to the Christian villages of Amboina, carrying for him his surplice and breviary and serving as his interpreter. The language was Malay. We are not told from what language Manuel was translating! Presumably he had some smattering of Portuguese. Xavier went from door to door in each of the villages with Manuel and asked about those who were ill and about children who had not been baptised. His coming consoled the Christians, who had been so long abandoned, and strengthened them in their in their faith against the lures and threats of their Muslim neighbours. Manuel later became the village chief of Hatiwi and was the champion of the Christians on Amboina during the persecution of 1558–61.

Xavier went to neighbouring islands, which were occupied by Alfuros, dreaded headhunters. One such island was Nusa Laut. The headhunters and their houses were adorned with the captured heads of their opponents. At times, they ate the flesh of their foes, whom they had slain in battle. The heels and arches of their feet, like their cheeks and hands, were deemed to be particular delicacies! (Schurhammer, Vol. III, p. 103). Xavier remained only a few days to preach the Gospel. His words found little reception among the inhabitants, partially because they had hardly any understanding of Malay. It was Xavier's first taste of complete apostolic failure – the language barrier was almost insuperable, and this time there was no interpreter. After about eight days he returned to Amboina. He spent just over three months on the island and is reckoned to have performed at least 400 baptisms each month.

Writing to his Jesuit companions in Europe from Amboina on 10 May 1546, Xavier mentions that he has cut their names from the letters which they had written to him '... so that I may constantly carry them with me with the vow of profession which I made because of the consolation which I received from them' Costelloe, pp. 139–44). When Xavier died he had a locket around his neck which contained a small relic of St Thomas, the formula of vows, and a signature of Ignatius which he had cut from a letter. In the same letter, Xavier also writes that he felt that he must go to the Islands of Moro in order to visit the abandoned converts, to baptise their children and to strengthen them in their faith. He knew that this would expose him to the danger of death since the people of those islands were notorious poisoners. Bermejo tells us (p. 143) that an added difficulty was that each island had its own language, and, at times, each town within the same island used a different dialect. The last priest who worked among them had been tricked and treacherously slain – a group of individuals invited him to come with them on a fishing expedition and when they reached the open sea they threw him overboard! Since then, no priest had dared to work among such savages, yet there were at least 10,000 baptised Christians among them. It seems that Xavier was determined to go, to help the thousands of Christians and to make new ones – it was always the double motive that drove him on. He was putting his life on the line, for he knew that he ran the risk of being killed and even eaten by the so-called Christians. As Bermejo writes, 'One can only wonder in amazement before such an incredible attitude of trustful hope' (p.145).

Ternate

Xavier went from Amboina to Ternate (in Indonesia), arriving in early July 1546. He was very well received by the Portuguese. The ignorance, especially among the native wives of the Christians, their male and female slaves, and the native Christians themselves was great. Xavier gave instructions in the faith for an hour twice a day to the children and adults. The result was that soon the boys, girls and women sang the Creed, Our Father, Hail Mary, Confiteor and the Commandments in the open squares and in their homes. At night, Xavier went with a small bell to the squares and urged all to pray for the souls in purgatory and for those who were living in mortal sin and refused to be converted. In Ternate, he devoted time to writing his only book, a very small book, amounting to fewer than five thousand words. Its subject was an exposition of the Apostles' Creed (Brodrick, p. 275). It was a brief catechism in verse, which could be memorised and then sung. One of the verses of Xavier's catechism is startling for us today: 'All those refusing to believe in Christ, the Moors, the Jews and the

Gentiles will go to hell – unsaved by Christ's redeeming grace' (Bermejo, p. 149). Bermejo puts this statement down to Xavier's hurried theology course in Paris. It is a far cry from the theology of the Second Vatican Council! (*Lumen Gentium,* 16).

The Islands of Moro

Notwithstanding the dangers mentioned above, Xavier sailed to the Islands of Moro (southern Philippines) with a few Portuguese companions. He wrote to his Jesuit companions in Rome of experiencing 'great consolations, so much so … that a man might well lose the sight of his bodily eyes within a few years from the abundance of his consoling tears. Never do I remember having had such great and continuous spiritual consolations as on these islands, or such little distress from physical labours. It would be better if they were called "Islands of Hope in God", rather than "Moro Islands"' (Costelloe, p. 172).

Xavier spent three months on the Islands of Moro (13 September to 13 December 1546). He took along a batch of boys from the Moro Islands who would be trained at St Paul's in Goa, and then return to evangelise their own people.

Return to Ternate

Xavier returned to Ternate where he lingered for another three months since Ternate was by far the most important town and island in the Moluccas. Before leaving (at Easter 1547), he made arrangements for the teaching of Christian doctrine twice a day. He had introduced, too, as in Malacca, the custom of sending a small procession through the streets at nightfall, headed by a member of the Confraternity of Mercy to pray aloud for the souls in Purgatory, and for all the persons in the town in a state of mortal sin (Brodrick, p. 284).

Back to Malacca

Xavier, along with João Eiró, returned to Malacca in July 1547. A large crowd had assembled on the beach after the news spread that the 'holy father' was coming. Sadly, on his return to Malacca, Xavier received a letter from Simon Rodrigues which told him of the death of his Jesuit confrère, Pierre Favre (+1546). Xavier was deeply affected by this news. He kept this letter as a last memorial of his former friend and as a precious relic.

Almost immediately after his return to Malacca, Xavier had taken up his usual labours in the hospital. He was occupied day and night and often went without eating regularly. Every afternoon he explained the teachings of the faith for two hours or more. Following the small catechism that he had composed in Ternate, his hearers learned twenty words a day from this rhymed work – they would have memorised the whole text in a year.

Xavier stayed in Malacca for close on five months. By December 1547, he had heard some definite news of Japan. The Portuguese had discovered Japan only five years earlier. A Japanese man, Anjiro, came to Malacca (Schurhammer, Vol. III, p. 271) and was brought to meet Xavier. Anjiro was around thirty-five years old and already spoke Portuguese. He was of a prominent family, a member of the warrior caste from southern Japan, where the Portuguese had been engaged in trade since the discovery of the Japanese Islands. He had two Japanese servants with him. They were able to tell Xavier much about Japan, assuring him that the Japanese showed a great thirst for knowledge.

Anjiro belonged to the Shingon Buddhist sect whose religious teachings entirely failed to give him the peace of soul for which he yearned. Brodrick tells us (p. 294) that Anjiro had a strongly developed sense of sin and longed to meet some master of the spiritual life who would help him to cope with his troubled conscience. He had a great longing to obtain knowledge of the truths of Christianity. He wrote down the articles of the Christian faith in his Japanese script. Xavier asked Anjiro if the Japanese would become

Christians if he went with him to Japan. Anjiro replied that the people of his land would not become Christians at once. They would first ask many questions to discover what the priest would reply and what he knew; and they would above all wait and see if he lived up to what he said. They were people who let themselves be guided by reason.

Xavier, therefore, fixed his plan. Within two years he or another priest would sail to Japan. Anjiro could, in the meantime, perfect his Portuguese at St Paul's in Goa. He could also translate the Christian doctrines and a detailed explanation of the articles of the Creed and of the history of the Incarnation into Japanese since he knew how to write this language so well.

Xavier made no move to baptise Anjiro, though the man came to him in the best disposition and already fairly well versed in Christian doctrine. Xavier could spend only a week in his company. He had to get back to India to clear up huge arrears of missionary business and to assign posts to eight new Jesuit arrivals.

Xavier left Malacca in mid-December 1547. Anjiro remained there with his two companions until the end of December, when he sailed for India.

Chapter 7

Back in Goa

Xavier landed in Goa on 6 March 1548 after an absence of almost four years. He found five new Jesuits – two priests and three scholastics – in St Paul's College. He also met Anjiro and his two companions.

Xavier's long absence from India meant that he was not well informed about the situation at St Paul's. The school, which now numbered around seventy students, was a confusion of races and languages. The students ranged in age from thirteen to twenty-one. Bermejo tells us (pp. 175–76) that by the age of twenty-five the students could be ordained and sent out. There was no selection process whatsoever, with the result that the standard was deplorably low. Nicolò Lancilotto complained to Rome that the students were 'real barbarians, aggressive and incapable of picking up whether doctrine or virtue … collected from different nations, one more barbarian than the other, from the most barbarous nations of the world.' He had no illusions about the moral climate of India and, as a consequence of his chronic illness (consumption), was inclined, as he knew himself, to a melancholic, pessimistic point of view. As far back as 1545, Lancilotto had complained to Rome that the boys were being half starved, partly to save expenses, and partly with the mistaken idea of hardening them for their future apostolate (Brodrick, p. 318).

On a more positive note, on Whit Sunday, 20 May 1548, Xavier had the joy of seeing his three Japanese friends baptised with great solemnity by the Bishop of Goa in his cathedral. Anjiro received the new name of Paul of the Holy Faith, his servant that of John, and the third man the name of Antonio. Antonio became completely attached to Xavier. In the five months of their stay in Goa the three had learned to read, write and speak Portuguese – they had been well instructed by Lancilotto.

In October 1548 Xavier made a brief visit to the Fishery Coast. The 'Great Father' was jubilantly received by the Paravas. During a visit in February 1548, Xavier had asked the native priest, Francisco Coelho, to translate into Tamil the catechism that he had composed in Ternate as an explanation of the articles of the faith, and Coelho had done this.

The Problem of Antonio Gomes SJ

On his return to Goa in the middle of November 1548, Xavier met Antonio Gomes for the first time. Gomes was only twenty-eight but was a full doctor in theology when he joined the Society in Portugal. His experience was very limited: he was only four years a Jesuit and had been ordained two years earlier. Simon Rodrigues had made Gomes rector of St Paul's, replacing Lancilotto who, for health reasons, was only too happy to hand over the reins of government. Rodrigues's confidence in Gomes seems to have been endless for, in addition to making him rector of St Paul's, he also made him Mission Superior of all the Jesuits in India, in Xavier's absence.

Gomes soon became known as a preacher extraodinaire. Schurhammer tells us (Vol. III, pp. 535–36) that Gomes was not only admired for his words and wisdom, but that his colloquies during his sermons were one single flood of tears – his own and those of his hearers! The Bishop of Goa, Frey Juan de Albuquerque invited Gomes to preach in the cathedral. It was impossible to satisfy all those who wished to go to confession as a result of his homilies.

Nevertheless, Antonio Gomes was Xavier's chief concern. There was no question that he was a learned theologian, a brilliant orator and, as a religious, a zealot for the law. However, as Bermejo mentions (p. 178), Gomes's exercise of authority became truculent, and in order to break all possible resistance and opposition, he claimed he had brought with him the necessary authority to arrest those who opposed him and send them back to Portugal in chains!

Gomes, according to Xavier, lacked two qualities: humility and charity – the humility to learn from others who knew India and its entirely different attitudes, and the charity to endure patiently the weaknesses and imperfections of his confrères and of the newly converted Indians. As Schurhammer relates (Vol. III, pp. 554–57), Gomes had taken up his office as rector like a second Savonarola, a merciless reformer who believed he had to teach his confrères the true spirit of the Institute of the Society of Jesus. He began to alter food and drink, sleep and study, prayer and Masses in both quantity and quality, and he imposed numerous mortifications.

Gomes also extended his reforms over the College of St Paul, taking over the spiritual and temporal administration of the college. He immediately began to revise everything: the order of studies was to be like that of Paris; prayer, meditation and examination of conscience were to be like those in Coimbra, Portugal, since he found the seventy or eighty native students restless, without spirit, and without devotion. Some of the students had clambered over the college wall and sought their salvation in hasty flight! This was the state of affairs when Xavier returned to Goa in the middle of November 1548. One month's experience in Goa had shown Gomes the way to secure the reform of the college and of the whole Indian mission!

The Indian boys, according to Gomes, disturbed the peace of the college since they had to be allowed to play! Sometimes they had to be whipped, and this caused the newcomers to become restless. The Indian boys should be sent away as soon as possible to a college somewhere else. The College of St Paul should be, and this was the opinion of Simon Rodrigues, who had discussed it with Gomes, exclusively for the philosophical and theological students of the Society. Apostolic schools could be opened elsewhere, where native boys could be taught reading, writing and Latin. When they had finished their schooling in these, those with less talent should be placed with *fidalgos* (nobles) or craftsmen, or employed as catechists. Those who were gifted and wished to continue their studies and showed signs of a vocation to the Society of Jesus should be sent to Goa.

Xavier wrote a letter to Ignatius in January 1549 asking that he (Ignatius) would appoint the next rector of the College (Costelloe, pp. 217–18). Three weeks later, Xavier wrote to Rodrigues telling him that he (Xavier) had dismissed Gomes from his position as rector and had appointed Gaspar Berze to be Superior of the College; Gomes could be free for preaching since he was much better at these tasks than that of ruling. (Costelloe, pp. 242–44). Xavier took the law into his own hands, transferred Gomes and coolly informed Simon Rodrigues of what he had done.

Bermejo relates (pp. 183–84) how Xavier planned to send Gomes to the extremely harsh mission of Hormutz in the Persian Gulf. Gomes cunningly secured the services of Cosme Anes, the founder of St Paul's, who requested that Xavier not remove Gomes from the rectorship. Nor were the people of Goa especially pleased since Gomes was Portuguese and Berze was from the Netherlands. Even the Bishop of Goa opposed the change since Gomes was a great preacher. Xavier had to retract. However, Xavier limited Gomes's authority as rector to the students of the college and to the Portuguese novices he had received into St Paul's. Gomes remained principal of the college, while Micer Paolo would be the Superior of all Jesuits in India. So, in the brief span of seven months (from September 1548 to April 1549), St Paul's had as many as four rectors (Lancilotto, Gomes, Berze and Micer Paolo).

Who was immediately responsible for appointing the rector of St Paul's, Ignatius in Rome, Francis in Goa or Rodrigues in Lisbon? Xavier himself seems to have been somewhat confused, for in his letter of January 1549 he asks Ignatius to send someone to be rector and, six months later, writing from Malacca, he asks Simon Rodrigues in Portugal to do exactly the same! Until Ignatius appointed Xavier full Provincial of the East, independent of Lisbon, there was no solution to be found (Bermejo, p. 184).

Indian Jesuits?

On a totally different matter, Xavier wrote to Ignatius in January 1549 touching upon the fundamental topic of Indian vocations to the Society: 'The native Indians in this part of the world are a race … very barbarous … and have no desire to learn anything … From experience which I have had here, I clearly see, my dearest Father, that our Society can in no way be perpetuated by native Indians' (Costelloe, pp. 216–218). One cannot but smile at this since, as recently as 2022, there were 3,955 Jesuits in India, including 199 novices. Xavier did not admit any Indians into the Society. The first Indian novice entered the Society only in 1561, nine years after Xavier's death. Bermejo suggests that Xavier's reluctance to admit Indians into the Society was perhaps understandable at the time, for the boys he met were still first-generation Christians, whose parents were often Hindus (Bermejo, pp.181–89).

Back in Cochin

Xavier left Goa and arrived in Cochin in mid-December, 1548. He spent two months there. He was able to do much good through his ardent preaching and his hearing of confessions. He visited the sick in the hospital, which almost became his second residence. When he saw a native lying ill and helpless on the street, he would wrap him in his cloak and carry him to the hospital, where he would take care of him.

In a letter to Ignatius from Cochin on 12 January 1549, Xavier writes:

> Because of the abundant information which I have on Japan, which is an island that is near China, and since there are no Moors or Jews in Japan but only pagans, and they are a race that is most inquisitive and eager to know what is new, both with respect to God and to other, natural things, I have with much interior satisfaction,

> decided to go to this land, for it seems to me that a people of this kind could by themselves continue to reap the fruit which those of the Society are producing during their lifetime. Xavier claims that the three Japanese men (Anjiro [Paul of the Holy Faith], John and Antonio) have provided us with a great amount of information on those regions of Japan and are individuals of upright manners and great talents, especially Paul. (Costelloe, pp. 219–223).

It is interesting that Xavier closes the above letter by addressing Ignatius as 'most reverend Father of my soul, as I kneel upon the ground while writing this as if I were in your presence … commend me much to God … in your prayers … that he may grant me to know his most holy will in this present life and give me the grace to fulfil it perfectly. Amen.' Xavier always had a profound regard for Ignatius.

In stark contrast, we see how bold, direct and fearless Xavier can be when writing to King John III of Portugal in a letter of 26 January 1549: 'Experience has taught me that Your Highness is not strong enough to spread the faith of Christ in India, though strong enough to take and possess all of India's temporal wealth … You will see yourself deprived of all your kingdom and lordships at the hour of death and entering others, where it will be something new for you to receive orders, and, may God avert it, to be expelled from paradise' (Costelloe, pp. 238–9).

On the Way to Japan

Xavier appears to have travelled between Goa and Cochin numerous times. He was in Goa at the beginning of April 1549 but was soon bound for Cochin again, on his way to Malacca. He left Goa for Cochin on 15 April, with the Spaniards Father Cosme de Torres and Brother Juan Fernández, the three Japanese, a Chinese man christened Manuel, and Amador, a Malabar servant. On

25 April they left Cochin for Malacca on the royal ship sailing for the Moluccas.

On 31 May, after a voyage of thirty-seven days, they arrived in Malacca. The Portuguese captain, Pedro de Silva, son of the legendary Vasco da Gama, succeeded in finding a Chinese merchant who was willing to take Xavier and his companions to Japan. Xavier remained in Malacca from 31 May until 24 June 1549. He departed for Japan on 24 June.

The crew of the flimsy vessel that was to take them to Japan was composed entirely of pagan Chinese. It carried 120 hundredweight of pepper as a gift for the king of Japan and a cask of Mass wine. Months later, Xavier would inform the Goan Jesuits about the dangers encountered during the journey (Costelloe, pp. 294–95). During a storm, the daughter of the captain fell into the sea and was drowned before her father's eyes. The pagan crew offered sacrifices to idols. Xavier wrote that such was the extent of pagan practice among the crew that it depended on a demon and his minions whether they went to Japan or not. Finally, neither the demon nor his minions could block Xavier's passage: 'God brought us to these lands [Japan] which we so ardently desired to reach' (Costelloe, p. 297).

Chapter 8

Japan

Kagoshima

On 15 August, 1549, Xavier and his companions landed in Kagoshima, the southernmost city of Japan. It was exactly fifteen years to the day since Xavier's first vows in faraway Paris. Kagoshima was the capital of the province of Satsuma (Kyûshû). Xavier and his companions were warmly received by the mayor of Kagoshima. They were guests in the home of Anjiro's mother, wife and daughter. Here, in the Land of the Rising Sun, the newcomers found themselves suddenly transported into an entirely new and exotic world. Men and women wore long, gaily coloured kimonos and carried brightly coloured fans and folding parasols. Men and boys, proud samurai (members of the warrior class) carried two-edged swords in lacquered black wooden sheaths at their belts.

In a long letter of November 1549 from Kagoshima to the Jesuits in Goa, Xavier writes:

'We have come here … that we may free the souls which for more than 1,400 years have been enslaved to Lucifer who has made himself be worshipped by them as God upon the earth, since he was unable to do this in heaven; and, after having been expelled from it, he takes revenge upon as many as he can, and also upon the sorry Japanese' (Costelloe, p. 310).

Here again is Xavier's theological stance, so widespread at the time, that outside the Church there is no salvation.

Xavier's first impressions of the Japanese were: 'As a race, they have very fine manners; and they are on the whole good and not malicious. They have a marvellous sense of honour and esteem it more than anything else … They are temperate in eating, though they are somewhat excessive in drinking. They drink wines made from rice, since there are no vines in these regions. They swear little and when they do swear, it is by the sun … They do not have more than one wife … They have a profound abhorrence of the vice of theft' (Costelloe, pp. 297–98).

The customs of the people were also strange. The left was the place of honour, white was the colour of mourning. Guests to a home were welcomed with numerous bows and entertained with little bowls of bitter tea, the Japanese national drink, and sweet cakes. Food was carried to the mouth with two chopsticks, a skill that could be learned only with repeated practice.

Xavier went with Anjiro as his interpreter to visit Duke Shimazu Takashisa of Ijuin, four hours north-west of Kagoshima. Xavier presented the duke with a beautifully decorated bible. The duke granted them permission to preach the new doctrine and offered them material support. He lent them a little house in Kagoshima, where they took up residence: Xavier, Torres, Fernández, the two servants, the Chinese Manuel and the Malabar Amador, and probably Anjiro's two companions, Antonio and John.

Anjiro's mother, wife and daughter and many of his relatives and friends, both men and women, became Christians; and since many of them could read and write, they quickly learned the prayers. The first one to become a Christian outside this group was a poor young man of the warrior caste, a samurai who had been born in Kagoshima. He had received the name Bernardo in baptism. He became very attached to Xavier. He was humble, pious, devoted to prayer and eager for knowledge, and he consequently made great progress in the Christian faith. In addition to Bernardo, there was the owner of the house that the duke had designated as the residence for Xavier and his companions in Kagoshima. She was baptised with the name Maria and was from then on a zealous Christian.

Bernardo would be the first Japanese person to visit Europe. He was eventually received into the Society of Jesus in Lisbon and travelled through Salamanca, Barcelona and Naples to Rome in 1555, three years after Xavier's death. Ignatius Loyola had summoned Bernardo to Rome. Bernardo died at a relatively young age in Coimbra, Portugal.

One insuperable obstacle stood in the way to further conversions: the language. In his long letter to Goa, Xavier writes: 'If we knew the language we would gain much fruit … We are now learning the language like little children … We are now like so many statues among them, since they speak and talk about us, while we, not understanding their language, are mute' (Costelloe, p. 306). When Anjiro was talking with his visitors, Xavier and his companions had to remain silent. After spending forty days learning Japanese with Anjiro's assistance, Xavier was able to explain the Ten Commandments in the language of the country.

The *Bonzes*

The city of Kagoshima was known for its many temples and *bonzes* (*bôzu* in Japanese – the word *bonze*, basically meaning 'monk', was introduced by Xavier into Europe). Kagoshima lay in the most conservative provinces of Japan and the practice of the old Shinto religion was evident in the numerous shrines of the gods.

Anjiro spoke to Xavier about the monastery of Fukusho-ji of the Zen sect and Xavier visited it soon after his arrival in Kagoshima. He became more familiar with it than with any other site in the city. About a hundred monks lived in this Buddhist monastery, which was ruled by Ninshitsu, a sort of abbot. One day Ninshitsu took Xavier to the prayer hall where the monks were engaged in silent meditation. Xavier enquired what they were doing, and the abbot, with a smile said, 'Some are counting up how much they received during the past months from the faithful; some others are thinking about where they can obtain better clothes and food … others are thinking about their recreations and amusements; in short, none of them is thinking about anything that has any bearing at all' (Schurhammer, Vol. IV, p. 74).

Among the visitors who came to see Anjiro, Xavier and his companion priests, there were many *bonzes* who were interested in the new teaching of the foreigners. The *bonzes* were very numerous and were powerful in the city. They abused boys in the monastery for sinful purposes, as they openly admitted. The laymen agreed with Xavier and his companions when they condemned these unnatural sins as a severe offence against God. But the vice was so general and so deeply rooted that the *bonzes* were not reproached for it. Xavier did reproach them, warning them to avoid this ugly vice of sexual abuse of the boys; but the *bonzes* did not take his reproofs seriously. They simply laughed them off without showing any shame for their sins.

Notwithstanding their obvious vices, Xavier wrote to the Jesuits in Goa: 'A large number of Japanese are bonzes, who are greatly obeyed in the land where they live, even though their sins are manifest to all. The reason why they are held in such high regard, it seems to me, is the fact that they are very abstemious: they never eat fish or flesh, but only vegetables, fruits and rice, and these only once a day and with great moderation; they are given no wine' (Costelloe, p. 308).

Xavier would later write from Cochin on 29 January 1552 to the Jesuits in Europe: 'The people themselves are fully convinced that these bonzes … have the power to save souls that are going to hell, since they have bound themselves to keep the commandments and to recite other prayers in their stead … It is painful to write about the deceits preached by these bonzes. They never give alms, but they want to receive them from everyone else …' (Costelloe, pp. 329–30).

Xavier's principal work in Kagoshima during the winter of 1549–50 was the instruction of the Christians, the study of Japanese and especially the drafting of a lengthy exposition of Christian doctrine in Portuguese for Paul to translate into Japanese. Xavier had brought with him from India his 'shorter catechism', containing the prayers, the Creed and the Ten Commandments – that too was translated by Anjiro. No trace of either work in its Japanese form has survived. The main difficulty was to find Japanese words for Christian concepts. The translation of the book was imperfect. Anjiro had not received a higher education, and despite all his good intentions, the work was so defective that it badly represented the thoughts of Xavier and its style offended the educated. In addition, there was the poor pronunciation and unusual gestures of Xavier and the new, curious and unintelligible doctrine that he presented. Some of his hearers ridiculed him, others laughed, others said that he was crazy. Xavier did not let himself be deterred by the scoffers.

By the summer of 1550, the status of the mission in Kagoshima had worsened. The *bonzes* of Kagoshima encouraged the growing suspicions of the duke – the *daimyo*, himself a good Buddhist. They had perceived the incompatibility of the new teaching with their own and the danger that it posed for them. It was due to the influence of the *bonzes* that the number of converts, which in the first months of Xavier's stay in Kagoshima had amounted to around a hundred, had not reached 150 by the time of his departure for Hirado (in Nagasaki Prefecture). The *bonzes* insisted to the *daimyo* that if he permitted his vassals to accept the new religion, he would lose his lands, and their temples would be destroyed and abandoned by the people.

The *daimyo*, Takashisa, resisted the complaints of the *bonzes* for some time, since he hoped that the presence of foreign priests would attract to his harbour Portuguese ships, which brought so many precious wares and things that he needed in his wars with his enemies. But now he saw himself deceived in this regard. The Portuguese ships did not come as they had in the past, but had instead sailed to the harbour of his rival in Hirado. As a consequence, he finally yielded to the demands of the *bonzes* and forbade, on pain of death, any further conversion to the new religion.

Since no further development of the mission was possible at this time, Xavier decided not to wait any longer but, instead, to carry out his earlier plan of sailing to Miyako (modern-day Kyoto) from

Hirado in order to obtain permission to preach the Gospel from the king of Japan, and also to secure, if possible, an entrance into the famous university of Hieizan. Xavier handed over the care of the small Christian community in Kagoshima to Anjiro, his loyal companion and interpreter.

Hirado

Xavier was in Hirado from September to October 1550. There was a large Zen monastery of Yasmaduke there with a community of around a hundred. These did not preach but instead taught their meditations to the people and led an ostentatious, luxurious life. With the arrival of the Portuguese in Hirado, the local *daimyo*, Takanobu, readily gave the priests the permission they asked to preach their new doctrine in his land; and through the public reading of the book that had been composed in Kagoshima, and preaching (Brother Juan Fernández could already speak Japanese), around a hundred people became Christians within a short time. The first to be baptised by Xavier was his host, Antonio Kimura, who was then followed by his family into the new faith.

Yamaguchi

Xavier then decided to go to Yamaguchi, about 150 miles from Hirado. He took Bernardo and Fernández with him. Winter had already set in. The journey was nightmarish. There were pirates on the seas; snowstorms and icy winds. They were poorly clothed. Their legs swelled in the freezing temperatures. In villages, the children ran after them, pelting them with stones (Bermejo, p. 219).

Yamaguchi was one of the largest and most important cities in Japan. Besides the ordinary homes, there were many elaborate dwellings of the nobility, numerous Shinto shrines and Buddhist temples, and more than a hundred monasteries of *bonzes*. It was almost as large as Lisbon. The powerful *daimyo*, Ōuchi Yoshitaka, was one of the most powerful princes in Japan, ruling over six provinces. He was devoted to idolatry and magical practices. Xavier and his friends were put up at a hostelry owned by a man named Uchida.

Xavier and Fernández went in their poor clothes to Yoshitaka's palace. Fernandez read the chapters of the book on Creation and the Commandments. He also read about the sin of Sodom, where it said that a person who engaged in such shamefulness was filthier than a pig and meaner than a dog and other irrational animals! This passage seemed to strike deeply into the conscience of the duke, and his face betrayed the fact that he was upset by this teaching. He gave a sign that Xavier and Fernández should leave. Fernández thought that they would be killed but they were allowed to go (Schurhammer, Vol. IV, p. 162).

Since nothing happened to them, they calmly continued with their street preaching without any visible success. One day it happened that when Fernández was preaching, one of his hearers, in order to deride him, spat in his face. Without betraying the least emotion, Fernández quietly drew out his handkerchief, wiped the spittle from his face as if it was perspiration and continued with his preaching. This heroic self-control made such an impression on one of those present that he asked for baptism – the first in Yamaguchi. It was Uchida, their host, who received the sacrament with his whole family. However, other conversions were few and, eight days before Christmas, Xavier, Fernández and Bernardo left Yamaguchi in order to continue their journey to Miyako, the imperial city (Schurhammer, Vol. IV, pp. 162–63).

Miyako

It had been the coldest time of year when Xavier and his companions left Yamaguchi. Xavier went barefoot, even though the snow was frequently so deep that it reached their knees. Miyako was the capital of Japan and the residence of the emperor or supreme ruler of all Japan. Xavier wished to achieve two things in Miyako:

to speak with the emperor to obtain permission to preach, and to visit the University of Hiei-zan in order to herald the faith there, to dispute with the scholars of that institution and to obtain their approval for the public expression of his teaching. Hiei-zan was the chief site of Buddhist sects and scholars. It boasted more than 500 monasteries. Xavier saw it as a counterpart to the University of Paris. In order to obtain an audience with the *zasu* , its superior, a rich gift, was required, and since Xavier had left all his treasures in Hirado, his efforts to enter Hiei-zan were to no avail. The companions quickly returned to Miyako.

When Xavier visited the emperor's palace with his companions, he was bitterly disillusioned. The city manifested the devastating consequences of the preceding wars. The royal palace was a ramshackle, wooden building surrounded by a bamboo stockade. The emperor lived without pomp or a royal court, and was largely secluded from the world. The *shoguns* in the long past had deprived the emperor of his imperial powers, and then the *daimyos*, whom they had created and ennobled, proceeded to clip the wings of the *shoguns*. Xavier was soon to learn that the emperor (Õ – Vo) was no more than a figurehead who only appeared in public on certain festivals. Xavier was refused admission here too.

During the ten or eleven days that Xavier stayed in Miyako, he tried to preach on the streets but he discovered that the land was not ready for this. There were ominous signs of a renewed outbreak of civil war.

Back to Yamaguchi

Xavier had a plan to return to the *daimyo* in Yamaguchi, Õuchi Yoshitaka, no longer as a poor man of Christ, but with his letters of introduction and gifts, for Japan did not understand the poverty of the cross. Xavier went to the palace dressed in silk as an ambassador of the governor of India, Garcia de Sà, and as a representative of King John III of Portugal and Bishop Albuquerque who, in turn, represented Pope Julius III. The introductory letters were written on magnificently illuminated parchments.

Xavier also presented Yoshitaka with thirteen precious gifts, which Garcia de Sà and Dom Pedro da Silva, the captain of Malacca, had consigned to him for the Emperor of Japan (Schurhammer, Vol. IV, pp. 218–19). Xavier unpacked gifts never seen before in Japan: a beautiful clock that chimed the hours day and night; a musical box; two spectacles with which old people with dimmed eyesight could see clearly again; a fine glass mirror; an elaborate musket with three barrels; several bales of fine brocade; books richly bound in the European style; some beautiful crystal vases; several pictures in oils; two telescopes and an unstated quantity of port wine (Bermejo, p. 234).

Yoshitaka was delighted with the gifts and letters and readily granted Xavier's request to allow him to preach the law of God in his land and let those who wished to receive it do so. He gave them an empty *bonze* monastery for their dwelling. Their new dwelling was filled from morning to evening with curious visitors – nobles, *bonzes* of all sects, magicians, merchants and others. Endless questions were asked. Some of the nobles became Christians – a large proportion of the neophytes were of the samurai class.

The first audience with Yoshitaka was followed by a second. This time Xavier brought a very rich, beautifully illuminated bible and a new, beautifully decorated *Glossa ordinaria* (a commentary on Sacred Scripture). He told Yoshitaka that all the holy law was contained in these books. Yoshitaka also wished to see the brocaded vestment that Xavier had brought with him. He asked Xavier to put it on. The sight of it pleased him so much that he clapped his hands and said, 'This priest actually looks like a living image of our gods' (Schurhammer, Vol. IV, p. 223).

At first glance there might seem to have been reminders of Christianity among the Japanese *bonzes* – prayer beads, incense, vestments, bells, sacrifices and ceremonies. Dainichi, the main god of the Shingon sect, was, at times, represented with three heads, but without a body. Was this somehow an image of the Trinity? It would be very naive to think so. The *bonzes* were, in fact, totally ignorant of Christian faith, prayer and liturgical practices.

Xavier asked the *bonzes* about the mystery of the Trinity and the relations that existed between the Divine Persons, and whether they also believed and preached that the Second Person of the Blessed Trinity had assumed flesh and had become a man and died upon the Cross in order to save humankind.

These matters were completely unknown to the *bonzes*. They seemed to them to be dreams and fables. Some even laughed at what they heard from Xavier. Xavier became suspicious of the name Dainichi (literally 'the Great Sun'), learning from some of his new converts that Dainichi was not a personal God. Xavier immediately ordered Fernández to cry out in the streets, 'Do not worship Dainichi!' and to preach that he should not be honoured as God. From then on, in order to avoid any misunderstanding, Xavier used only the Latin word *Deus* for God, which was pronounced by the Japanese as *Deusu*.

Friendship with the Shingon *bonzes* was now a thing of the past. They refused to see Xavier or to let him into their monasteries. The controversies were for the most part centred on hell. This was the focal point of the sermons of the *bonzes* and something that they repeatedly stressed. They preached that they could save their benefactors from hell if they should happen to go there. They should therefore honour their *bonzes* and give alms to them. In his preaching Xavier spoke out against this and declared that this claim was a lie. The *bonzes* were enraged. They stirred the people up against the foreign preachers. Their *Deusu* could only be a great demon and the foreign preachers were his disciples. *Deusu* was *Daiuso*, that is, 'the Great Lie'.

The more the *bonzes* became enraged, the more the Christians increased in numbers. Within two months there were already 500 of them and others were added every day, chiefly from the people at court and officials of Yoshitaka. The conversion of one former *bonze* caused a sensation. The man was considered to be the most learned man in Yamaguchi. He said that he no longer believed in the religions of Japan. Xavier also baptised a street musician, blind in one eye and half blind in the other, and employed him as an interpreter and catechist. He was given the name of Lawrence. Eventually, he was the first Japanese person to be received as a lay brother into the Society.

There was a particular issue that still troubled the new converts. In a letter to his companions in Europe, written from Cochin on 29 January 1552, Xavier tells us of their concern: 'If God was so merciful, why had God not revealed himself to their ancestors before priests arrived from Europe? … If it was true (as we said) that those who did not adore God all go to hell, God had no mercy on their ancestors. This was one of the great doubts' (Costelloe, pp. 334, 335, 345). The new converts felt sorry for their deceased parents, wives, children, relatives and friends; and they asked Xavier if those in hell could not be freed from it through prayers and alms. Xavier told them that no one could be redeemed from hell, grieved as he was when he saw them weeping for their dead. Here, again, we see Xavier's harsh theology of salvation of non-Christians. This theology is a long way from that of *Lumen Gentium* 16: 'Those also attain salvation who through no fault of their own do not know the gospel of Christ or his Church, yet sincerely seek God and, moved by grace, strive by their deeds to do his will as it is known to them through the dictates of conscience' (Walter Abbott [ed.], *The Documents of Vatican II,* p. 35).

In August 1551, news came that a Portuguese ship had landed in Bungo on the north-eastern coast of Kyüshü (the third largest island of Japan's five islands). The journey there from Yamaguchi usually took five to seven days. Xavier left Anjiro in charge of the Kagoshima Christians until such time as he could provide a priest for the little flock. Cosme de Torres would be that priest.

Bungo

As soon as Otomo Yoshishige, the Duke of Bungo, learned of Xavier's arrival, he invited him to visit his palace. Xavier was received with the highest honours by the duke and it made a great impression on his courtiers when the Portuguese spread their precious cloaks on the mat-covered floor so that Xavier could sit upon them. Yoshishige wished to conclude a treaty of friendship with the king of Portugal. He listened with interest to Xavier when he spoke of the Christian faith. He gladly gave permission to preach in his land and he had a residence provided for Xavier in Okinohama (now the second largest city in Japan), where the ship of Duarte da Gama was lying at anchor and the Portuguese were selling their wares.

In the meantime, Xavier's first care was for the Portuguese on the ship. He offered Mass for them, heard their confessions and those of their Christian slaves and prepared them for the reception of Holy Communion. Duarte da Gama gave an excellent example to his men and maintained strict discipline on his ship. Xavier was greatly consoled by his work among the Portuguese.

Departure for India

Xavier decided to sail from Bungo to India in order to visit his confrères there, to take any measures that might be needed, to select suitable missionaries, and to sail back to Japan the following year with them. In November 1551, he set sail towards Malacca and Cochin. He took Bernardo and three other Japanese with him and arrived in Cochin on 24 January 1552.

After setting things right in India he would come back to Japan. That was the plan.

Not long after Xavier's departure for India, Cosme de Torres was able to baptise about 2,000 Japanese, but then a new armed rebellion forced him to flee. The missionaries had only escaped death as if by miracle. Yamaguchi was captured by rebels and was burned to the ground. The *daimyo*, Yoshitaka, committed hara-kiri. There came an era of bloody martyrdom. At least twenty-two Christians from Yamaguchi were beheaded, burned or crucified. Scarcely fifty years after Xavier's missionary activity, the total number of martyrs reached several thousands. Today, the Church celebrates the feast of twenty-six Japanese martyrs of Nagasaki and another 205 blessed who perished in the seventeenth century.

On the voyage to Sancian and Malacca the ship encountered a fierce storm at sea. Four sailors were thrown overboard in a sloop (small boat). They were given up as drowned but Xavier insisted that the ship be stopped to search for them. He gave himself up to prayer. Eventually, the four sailors were spotted and saved. Two of the four sailors rescued were Muslims and they were so impressed they became Christians. At Xavier's beatification process in Malacca, Goa, Cochin and Lisbon, there were sixty-one witnesses who testified to this event (Schurhammer, IV, pp. 301–305).

Chapter 9

Malacca and Goa

Back in Malacca

Xavier had not received any correspondence from Europe since 1548. When he returned to Malacca from Japan at the end of 1551 he found a good number of letters from both Europe and India. Among these was one from Ignatius, dated 10 October 1549. Ignatius wrote, 'Since we have the greatest confidence in your piety and prudence, which is in Christ Jesus, we make and appoint you provincial superior of all of ours who are in India and in other regions across the sea which are subject to the most serene king of Portugal and beyond them' (Costelloe, p. 290). The last three words are added perhaps because Japan was not among the lands subject to the Portuguese king. Thus Ignatius separated the province of the East from Portugal. So, Xavier was to be Provincial of the East, that is, of all the lands beyond the Cape of Good Hope as far as China and Japan.

Ignatius concluded another letter to Xavier with the words, 'Entirely yours without my ever being able to forget you, Ignatio.' Xavier later confessed to Ignatius in a letter written from Cochin, dated 29 January 1552, 'I read these words with tears, so I am writing these with tears, as I recall times past and the great love which you had, and still have for me' (Costelloe, pp. 344–45). Here we see the passionate side of Xavier, how much he valued the friendship of his companions, though he was to spend so much of his missionary activity alone.

Xavier had arrived in Malacca on 27 December 1551. His missionary activity in Japan had come to an end. He would never see Japan again. In all, he had spent twenty-seven months there. Three days after arriving in Malacca he set sail for India on Antonio Pereira's *Galega*. During the voyage he read his correspondence. He learned that almost three years earlier Antonio Criminali, Superior of the Fishery Coast, had been murdered. He had been attacked by the Badagas, enemies of the Portuguese Christians. Criminali was the first Jesuit martyr.

Return to Goa

The *Galeaga* arrived in Cochin on 24 January 1552 and, after a brief stop, pushed on to Goa. By the middle of February, Xavier was back at St Paul's. There were now thirty-nine confrères in the college. Among these were seven priests and nine brothers whom Xavier had known previously. Nine more who had come from Portugal in 1551 he now saw for the first time. There were also some new scholastics.

Xavier's first concern on arriving in Goa was the question of the rector of the College and the superior of the mission. There was no question of Antonio Gomes being suitable for the office. During Xavier's absence in Japan, Gomes had destroyed the college. With the support of the Governor Cabral, but against the statutes of the college, against Cosme Anes and its other founders, against the bishop and the people, against his confrères, Gomes had turned out upon the street all the native pupils, including the Paravas, and the students whom Xavier had chosen in the Moluccas (Schurhammmer, Vol. IV, p. 478). He had done this in order to take in Portuguese as candidates for the Society. Bermejo tells us (p. 258) that these candidates were all grown-up men who, however, could hardly read or write and had, therefore, no higher education at all. Gomes had radically altered the nature of the college, which had originally been set up exclusively for the training of

Indian boys for the secular priesthood, whereas Gomes had turned the institution into a Jesuit novitiate.

The general opinion was that Gomes was an excellent preacher but entirely unsuitable for governance (Bermejo, p. 259). There was a serious charge of financial mismanagement against him – the revenues of the college had not been intended for the use of the Society, but exclusively for the training of Indian boys, with the Society as the administrator, not the owner of the college. Gomes brushed all these objections aside, claiming that the king of Portugal would explicitly authorise what he was doing. In fact, the king's viceroy in India, Dom Afonso de Noronha, forced Gomes to accept again the dismissed Indian students.

The Jesuit Affonso Texeira often heard Xavier say of Gomes, 'Arrogance! Arrogance! The ruin you have caused, are causing and will continue to cause! And how opposed you are to the institute and perfection of the Society of Jesus' (Schurhammer, p. 509). He exhorted his brother Jesuits to strive for true interior humility, and he warned them against the dangers of arrogance.

Before leaving for Japan again, Xavier had Gomes banished to the isolated fortress of Diu, a God-forsaken spot 180 miles north-west of present-day Mumbai. Later, upon learning of Gomes's situation, Ignatius had his secretary, Juan de Polanco, write to Gaspar Barzaeus, the new rector of the college, that it would be as well for Gomes to return to Europe so that he could give an account of himself, since he had been held in such esteem as a preacher in India. On 1 February 1554, Gomes sailed from Cochin for Europe, but perished in the wreck of the *São Bento* during a storm east of the Cape of Good Hope.

Gaspar Barzaeus was the only one Xavier could consider for the offices of rector of St Paul's and vice-provincial. Barzaeus had arrived in Goa in November 1550, having received two more candidates into the Society in Ormuz (the strait between the Persian Gulf and the Gulf of Oman). While in Goa, Xavier had each of his new confrères come to him so that he might ask them about their previous lives and give them pertinent advice for their spiritual progress. It was, however, Xavier's own example that had the most influence upon them all. He was called the *Padre Santo*, not only by the Christians, but also by the pagans and the Muslims who showed him their respect.

On 7 December 1552 (ironically four days after Xavier's death), the Jesuit Melchior Nunes Barreto wrote the following of Xavier to his confrères from Bassein (in Maharashtra State, a Portuguese fort next in importance to Goa):

> ... his conversation is in heaven, though he walks here below ... what a heart so afire with the love of God! With what flames it is burning with love for his neighbour! O what zeal for helping souls that are sick or dead! ... he is a servant of Christ and of the sinner ... O what affability he has, always smiling with a calm and cheerful face, always smiling but never laughing; always smiling because he has ever a spiritual joy ... And still he never laughs, since he is always self-recollected, and he never abandons himself to creatures. (Schurhammer, Vol. IV, p. 501)

Xavier used to go to the community chapel in St Paul's. There he would remain for hours in prayer, until, overcome with weariness, he fell asleep where he was. At times, at night, he would walk in the college garden as he meditated with his eyes raised towards the heavens, much like Ignatius did in Rome.

Along with his love of the Crucified Christ and his reverence for the Blessed Trinity, Xavier had a devotion to the Blessed Virgin. He openly wore a rosary about his neck. He closed his instructions to the Christians with a prayer to Mary. He visited her chapels wherever he went. He carried her image to Japan. Like his Jesuit companion, the now deceased Pierre Favre, Xavier also had a great devotion to the angels. He taught that people should recommend themselves to their guardian angel. He chose St Michael the Archangel as the patron of his Japanese mission.

While he was at St Paul's, Xavier asked a novice to report, 'to pay attention to my failings; ask the others about them and come back and tell them to me'. The sixteen-year-old novice, Francisco Durão, took Xavier at this word, and with disarming simplicity repeated to him, 'They say, Father, that Your Reverence is a saint, but that you say Mass too quickly!' (Bermejo, p. 282). I would like to think that Xavier smiled at the good novice's honesty!

Xavier used to write to his Jesuit subjects that without true, prompt and joyful obedience one could not be a true son of the Society nor persevere in it with joy, merit and consolation. Their obedience should be prompt not only to their own religious superiors but also to secular authorities; and he used to say that it was much safer to obey and to be ruled than to command and to let oneself be led by one's own judgement and discretion. He also told, and even ordered, superiors to correct and punish those who failed to obey in any way (Schurhammer, Vol. IV, p. 520).

Xavier was rigorous on the point of religious obedience and on the danger of dismissal from the Society for the recalcitrant. One example is the case of Alvaro Ferreira, a Jesuit scholastic residing in Goa who was destined for Japan and was making good progress in learning Japanese. Suddenly, Xavier changed his appointment and decided that Ferreira should accompany him to China. When they were within reach of the Chinese coast, Ferreira lost courage as a consequence of certain frightening reports regarding the conditions in Chinese jails. Ferreira begged Xavier to be excused. Xavier immediately dismissed Ferreira from the Society!

In a letter to Father Gonçalo Rodrigues in Ormutz, dated 22 March 1552, Xavier reprimands him severely for the 'faults and impediments for which you yourself are responsible … Take care not to do anything for which you would be dismissed … remember how much greater need you have of the Society than the Society of you.' Then, after such harsh words, Xavier adds, 'I am writing you these lines because of my love for you and the good I wish you' (Costelloe, p. 362).

In a further letter to Father Melchior Nunes Barreto in Bassein, dated 3 April 1552, Xavier writes, '… see to it that you immediately dismiss from the Society those who are caught in public sins and are a source of scandal to the people' (Costelloe, p. 367).

To Father Alonso Cipriano in Mailapur, in a letter of 6 April 1552, Xavier writes, 'You have very poorly carried out the instruction that I gave you on what should be done in San Thomé … You are now so accustomed to doing your own will that, no matter where you are, you offend everyone with your way of acting … at the hour of your death you will have reason for regret.' Then, ironically, it might appear to us, Xavier writes, 'O Cipriano! If you knew the love with which I am writing these things to you, you would remember me both day and night, and you would perhaps weep as you remembered my great love for you. If the hearts of men could be seen in this life, believe me, my brother Cipriano, you would clearly see yourself with my soul' (Costelloe, pp. 392–94). Despite his rough character, Cipriano, in fact, was a man of solid virtue. He died in San Thomé in 1559, venerated as a saint. Melchior Nunes Barreto wrote of him, 'He was a most sincere and zealous man, although at times very sharp; but his virtues and his works of charity were so much greater that, when he died, the Christians and pagans wept for him' (Costelloe, p. 394).

It is striking to read a letter that Xavier wrote to Ignatius from Cochin on 12 January 1549, describing the qualities that the future rector of St Paul's should have: 'He must be affable and calm … and not severe … so that they [his confrères] do not gain the impression that he wishes to exact obedience through severity or servile fear. For many, if they perceive that he rules with severity and intimidation will leave the Society' (Costelloe, p. 217). This opinion prompts Bermejo to comment, 'This was surely admirable advice – apparently meant for others, not for Xavier himself!' (p.270).

It has to be admitted that this stress on total obedience and the threat of immediate dismissal from the Society are very unattractive qualities in Xavier. In all, he dismissed ten men, and, since at the time the Society had only about fifty-five members in the whole of the East, this means that a hefty 18 per cent of the total membership was dismissed by him. I agree with Bermejo that Xavier's methods were too harsh. 'One single act of disobedience, real or alleged, was enough for him to come down heavily on his subject and throw him out. He could be merciless. He never blamed himself. He was governing his men ... nearly always from thousands of miles away. He does not seem to have learned that the primary rule of any Superior is *personal* contact with his men. More than a compassionate father, at times, he resembles a military commander who rules with an iron hand' (Bermejo, p. 270).

On 6 April 1552, Xavier appointed Father Gaspar Barzaeus as rector of the College of St Paul and as Vice-Provincial. One of the phrases that keeps recurring in Xavier's letter to Barzaeus is, 'I order you in virtue of holy obedience ...'. Xavier continues, 'Every violation of obedience ... should be followed by a punishment and penance ... Treat with more severity than affability those whom you perceive ... to have a contempt for obedience; and assign them a penance' (Costelloe, p. 403).

There is an interesting letter from Xavier to Ignatius, dated 9 April,1552. In this letter Xavier treats of the qualities he deems necessary in the Jesuits who might be sent to Japan:

> From what I have experienced in Japan the priests who are to go there to produce fruits in souls, especially those who are to go to the universities, have need of two things: the first is that they have been much tried and persecuted in the world and that they have much experience and have acquired a great deal of interior knowledge of themselves, since they will be more persecuted in Japan than they ever were perhaps in Europe ... they will always be persecuted by the priests of Japan ... They must also be learned in order to be

> able to answer the many questions that are posed by the Japanese. It would be well that they were good Masters of Arts, and it would certainly be no loss if they were dialecticians, so that they could catch the Japanese in contradictions when they dispute with them. It would be good also if they knew something about the celestial sphere, since the Japanese are delighted with learning about the movements of the heavens, the eclipses of the sun, the waxing and waning of the moon, and how they are produced. The explanation of such matters is a great help in gaining the good will of the people. (Costelloe, pp. 383–87)

It is quite obvious here that Xavier is writing from his own personal experience of his efforts at dialogue and ministry in Japan. Xavier signs off on this letter with the moving phrase, 'Your least son and farthest exiled. Francysco.'

By now Xavier had determined that he would go to China. He had received from the bishop of Goa a letter of recommendation for the king of China, written on parchment and illuminated with gold. There were also gifts of precious ornaments, carpets and altarpieces.

Those selected for the Chinese mission were Father Balthasar Gago (who later did marvellous work in Japan, rather than China); the scholastic Alvaro Ferreira, who had completed his noviceship two years previously and had his appointment abruptly changed by Xavier from Japan to China; a young Chinese man called Antonio (Antonio of the Holy Faith) who had spent eight years at St Paul's College and was to act as interpreter, and a Malabar Christian named Christopher (Cristovão), in the capacity of a servant. During his time in St Paul's Antonio had studied Latin for four years.

Xavier left Goa on Easter Sunday, 17 April 1552 on the *Santiago*. Diogo de Sousa was the captain. While they were on their way to Malacca, Xavier had told the people on the *Santiago*, 'My sons,

Malacca is in great trouble.' They reached Malacca at the end of May. Xavier's premonition had not been wrong. In 1551, the Javanese, after giving up their siege of the city, had poisoned the 'Rajah Spring' from which Malacca obtained its drinking water, and had thus provoked a severe pestilence. Xavier visited the stricken day and night. From the *Santiago* alone some thirty-six had died

A further difficulty was that a man named Alvaro da Ataide had been appointed captain of the Malacca Strait, and, in that capacity, had complete control of all the shipping in and out of the harbour. For reasons of greed he impounded the *Santa Cruz*, the ship that was to carry Xavier to the Chinese coast.

As apostolic nuncio, Xavier drafted a document to be given to Ataide, threatening him with excommunication if he impeded the voyage. Ataide called Xavier a forger of papal documents. Unfortunately, Xavier had left behind him at Goa the precious parchment brief of Pope Paul III which had constituted Xavier apostolic nuncio in the East. Xavier wrote to João Soares, Vicar of Malacca, asking him to show Ataide the papal document of the Avignon Pope John XXII (1316–34), *Super Gentes*, which stated, '... the Roman Pontiff needs to send ambassadors to the nations and kingdoms ... Those who wish to impede the said ambassadors, or even nuncios, whom the See itself sends to whatever area and for whatever cause incur *ipso facto* a sentence of excommunication' (Costelloe, p. 423).

Attaide finally relented, but on his own terms. He permitted the *Santa Cruz* to sail, but manned by officers and sailors of his own choosing. Xavier left behind in Malacca the elaborate vestments and gifts that he had planned to present to the king of China. Six days after arriving in Malacca, Father Balthasar Gago left for Japan instead of China. Xavier was now the only priest on board the *Santa Cruz*. He was accompanied by Alvaro Ferreira, Antonio and his Malabar servant, Christopher.

Chapter 10

Sancian

It was about 1,500 statute miles from Malacca to the Chinese coast. The destination of the *Santa Cruz* was the little island of Sancian, lying just six miles off the Chinese mainland. Once on board ship, Xavier baptised sixty individuals – slaves, children of black slaves and Moorish sailors, heard the confessions of many and administered the sacraments. Xavier would spend the last three months of his earthly existence on the island of Sancian.

The Chinese Emperor Che Tsong (1522–1566) forbade foreigners entrance into his territories without his express written permission. Xavier, however, was determined to make his way to China at all costs.

There were other Portuguese ships in Sancian harbour. At Xavier's request some friendly Portuguese built him a small wooden hut covered with straw on the shore, together with a small church built out of straw mats. He offered Mass there every day. He instructed the children and slaves of the Portuguese. During the rest of the time he settled disputes, visited the sick and collected alms for the poor.

Writing to Father Francisco Pérez, in Malacca, on 22 October, 1552, Xavier tells him, 'After our arrival in Sancian, we built a church, and I said Mass every day until I became ill with fevers. I was sick for fifteen days; now, through the mercy of God, I have recovered my health. There has been no lack here of spiritual occupations, such as hearing confessions, visiting the sick, and reconciling enemies. I do not know anything more that I can tell you from here except that we are firmly resolved to go to China' (Costelloe, p. 442).

To Father Gaspar Barzaeus, in Goa, he writes on 25 October 1552, 'See to it that you do not readmit those whom I have dismissed and whom I have ordered you under obedience not to readmit … With respect to the services of the house, be careful to see if it would be better to acquire or buy some negroes for these services rather than to make use of the services of many who wish to enter the Society' (Costelloe, p. 446). Xavier plainly did not consider slavery to be contrary to Christian principles. (As late as 1866, when most world governments had already abandoned slavery as degrading and immoral, Pope Pius IX still defended its legitimacy – by appealing to Scripture.)

Xavier was above all concerned with finding an entrance into closed-off China. He consequently sought to gain the good will of the Chinese merchants who came from Canton in order to exchange their porcelain, lacquered wares and silks for the pepper and spices of the Portuguese. He hoped to find through them a Chinese merchant who would, for a suitable reward, be willing to carry him secretly to Canton in a ship. His efforts were in vain. The merchants replied that if the governor of the city learned about this, they would be putting their lives and possessions in the gravest danger. They refused to undertake the hazardous enterprise for any price.

One Manuel de Chaves, who had spent time in a Chinese jail, had some terrifying stories. He related how there were thousands of prisoners crowded together in filthy confinement. At night, their feet were stuck into large wooden blocks which made it impossible to sit or stand. Prisoners were beaten for the slightest excuse until they collapsed, streaming with blood. All of these stories made a deep impression upon the young scholastic Alvaro Ferreira, who was just recovering from an illness. He lost courage and declined to go to China. Xavier immediately dismissed him from the Society, and wrote to Father Francisco Pérez, in Malacca, on 12 November 1552, 'I have dismissed Ferreira from the

Society since he is not suited for it. I, therefore, order you in virtue of holy obedience not to receive him into the house in Cochin. Help him in every way to become a friar; help him with the friars of St Francis or of St Dominic' (Costelloe, p. 49).

On 13 November 1552, the Portuguese burned their huts and sailed south. They took with them Alvaro Ferreira and the last letters that had been written by Xavier.

Xavier was determined to go to China in spite of everything, without a confrère, and only with his Malabar servant, Christopher, and Antonio. The Chinese merchant who eventually agreed to take Xavier to Canton was to arrive on 19 November. Daily, and even hourly, Xavier watched out for him anxiously, but he did not come on the appointed day, nor the following.

Xavier fell seriously ill again on 21 November. Antonio heard him calling out, 'Jesus, Son of David, have mercy on me! O Mary, Mother of God, remember me!' Since he now felt that his death was near, Xavier ordered Antonio to take all his possessions – books, letters, clothes and pictures – immediately to the *Santa Cruz*.

Chapter 11

Death and Burials

Xavier died of pleurisy before dawn on Saturday 3 December 1552 on the island of Sancian, in a straw hut that was not his own, ten years after he had come to the regions of India. In his last agony he often said, 'Jesus, Son of David, have pity on me.' He died muttering in his own native Basque. He was forty-six.

Antonio went to the *Santa Cruz* for the vestments that Xavier had used for celebrating Mass so that he might be laid out in them for his burial. Because of the great cold, only four persons were present for the burial – Antonio, two enslaved men of mixed race, one of whom was Jorge Mendes, and a Portuguese, about whom nothing is known. After they had dug the grave and were about to place the coffin in it, one of them suggested to Antonio that it would be good to bury the body with a large amount of lime so that it would consume the flesh and make it easier to transfer the bones to India (Schurhammer, Vol. IV, pp. 643–44).

In the middle of February 1553, the *Santa Cruz* was being readied for its return voyage to Malacca. Xavier's body had by this time been buried for two-and-a-half months. The captain of the ship, Diogo Vaz de Aragão, sent a Portuguese to open the grave to ascertain the condition of the body. To his astonishment, the man found the body perfectly fresh and incorrupt and it was brought on board ship.

The *Santa Cruz* reached Malacca on 22 March 1553. News of the body's preservation spread throughout the city. On the following day there was a great procession from the harbour to the church of the Jesuits, Nossa Senhora do Monte. Xavier's body was buried in the nave of the church in front of the altar, but without lime.

Ironically, Ignatius wrote a letter to Xavier on 28 June 1553, almost seven months after his death.

> It seems to me that it would have been proper for you to have sent Master Gaspar [Barzaeus] and others to China … from what can be understood from here, I am of the opinion that God our Lord would have been better served by your person if you had remained in India and had sent others there, instructing them to do what you have done: for in this way you would have been doing in many places what you did through your own person in one, And I further say that, considering the greater service of God our Lord and the assistance of souls in those regions, and how much their welfare depends upon Portugal, I have decided to order you in virtue of holy obedience to take, among so many roads, the one leading to Portugal with the first opportunity that you have good voyage; and I am consequently ordering you to do this in the name of Christ our Lord, even though you should be ready to return soon to India … When … the king of Portugal is informed about affairs there by someone possessing such close personal knowledge as you do, you can easily imagine that he would be moved to do many things for the service of God and for the assistance of those regions about which you might report to him … Further, it is very important that the Apostolic See should have complete and definite information about the things of India, and from a person who is esteemed by it, so that it can provide the spiritual things that are needed or are very important for the good of both the new and old Christians who are living there … When you reach Portugal, you will be under the obedience of the king for doing

whatever he will require of your person for the glory of God our Lord. (Costelloe, pp. 456–458)

Meanwhile, Xavier's body lay in the earth for nearly five months, until the Feast of the Assumption in 1553. News of his death had by now reached India. Father João de Beira, who was then in Goa, rushed to Malacca to verify the news. He sought the help of Diogo Pereira, who had already organised the honours paid to his dead friend. Secretly, and at dead of night by the light of a lantern, the two men, helped by a few trusted companions, exhumed the body again and found it still wearing the colours of life. The body was taken to Pereira's house, where he reverently laid it in a coffin lined with Chinese damask and covered with fine brocade. Not until 11 December 1553, more than a year after Xavier's death, did a ship sail for India (Bermejo, p. 296).

Xavier's body arrived in Goa during the night of 15 March 1554. Thundering salutes from other ships greeted the body. The following day, the Friday of Passion Week, Xavier's remains were brought solemnly into the city. The Viceroy and others thought that the bells of the cathedral and of the other churches of the city should be rung. The Viceroy, cathedral chapter and members of the Confraternity of the Misericordia (founded around 1240 for assisting the ill and prisoners and burying the dead) took part in the solemn procession, together with ninety boys dressed in white cassocks and carrying lighted candles. The body was kept in a chapel of the College of St Paul. For four days the crowds thronged into the church to kiss the exposed feet. A Dominican priest preached at the funeral. A Jesuit named Aires Brandão who was present, said that the preacher could not be heard for the sobbing of the huge congregation and had to leave the pulpit, choked by his own tears (*Monumenta Xavieriana,* ii, 922–3, quoted in Brodrick, *St Francis Xavier,* p. 531).

Xavier's body was still intact and there were some people who suggested that it must have been embalmed. The Viceroy instructed the chief medical authority in the city to make a thorough examination of the corpse. A doctor, Cosmas de Saraiva, examined the body and swore on oath that there was no scientific or medical reason why the body should be so preserved (Bermejo, pp. 297–98).

In 1575, the first Provincial Congregation of the Jesuits in India wished to see Xavier's body transferred to a worthier sight. In 1582, it was brought to the chapel of the Jesuit novices at St Paul's' College. Xavier's nephew, Jerónimo Xavier, was the novice master at the time. In 1605, Xavier's body was transferred to the main chapel of the college. The body was later transferred to the Church of Bom Jesus, where it is still the object of great veneration.

In 1694, the shrine was again opened at the request of the newly consecrated Vicar Apostolic of the East, Espínola. The corpse had all the appearance of a living man. Only fourteen years later did the first signs of darkening and desiccation begin to appear.

The silver shrine where Xavier's relics are kept has been opened many times since then and, in 1932, permission was granted for the body to be photographed. By then it was definitely mummified. The severed arm has been in the Church of the Gesù in Rome for more than 300 years. From there it has been taken around the world and is an object of veneration for many.

Epilogue

Miracles and Canonisation

Only seventeen years after Xavier's death, the Jesuit Pedro Ribadeneira (1527–1611) published his life of Ignatius Loyola, in which he included a short chapter on Xavier. In this work, Ribadeneira asserts that Xavier received 'the gift to work many and illustrious miracles … He cured infirmities of many kinds … restored sight to the blind and raised the dead to life …' (Quoted in Bermejo, p. 298). There is no historical evidence that these miracles actually occurred.

Bermejo tells us (p. 299) that the Jesuit Alexandro Valignano (1539–1606), who worked on the missions in India, Macau and China, was clearly impatient of the series of miracles attributed to Xavier and demanded exact proof before accepting any of them. He wrote in January 1585 from Cochin to the Fifth Superior-General of the Jesuits, Father Claudio Aquaviva (1543–1615, Generalate, 1581–1615), 'Regarding the miracles and the manner of life attributed to Father Master Francis … some people speak of these things rather carelessly, exaggerating and magnifying according to their own inclination and credulity, whatever they pick up on the street' (Bermejo, p.265).

Bermejo observes (p. 300) that unfortunately the Vatican did not share Valignano's sensible opinion, for scarcely four decades afterwards, in the official Bull of Canonisation (12 March, 1622), fact and fiction are inextricably mixed together. Mention is made of Xavier's 'levitation' while saying Mass. He is alleged to have converted 'many hundreds of thousands', a wild claim that is a fantastic distortion of the facts and a gross exaggeration. Xavier is said to have 'often suffered shipwreck', which, in reality, he did not suffer even once. Most incredibly of all, the Bull states, 'suddenly taught by God several languages unknown to him, he spoke them fluently, as if he had been brought up in those regions … and sometimes it happened that the listeners understood him each in his own tongue' – a replica of the original Pentecost miracle in Jerusalem (Acts 2:1–12). In reality, despite his efforts, Xavier did not speak a single Oriental language. Besides his native Basque, he had a good command of Spanish and French and an adequate working knowledge of Italian, Latin and Portuguese. This leads Bermejo to assert in an endnote (p. 300) that 'on the whole and from the historical point of view, the Vatican Bull is a worthless document with no critical sense, whatsoever'.

Among the first petitioners for the beatification of Xavier was King John III of Portugal. In 1556, he ordered his Viceroy in India to gather testimonies of Xavier's life and virtues.

Xavier was beatified by Pope Pius V on 25 October 1619 and canonised by Pope Gregory XV on 12 March 1622, along with Saints Isidro of Madrid, Philip Neri, Ignatius Loyola and Teresa of Avila. Pope Benedict XIV (1740–58) constituted Xavier patron saint of India and of all the East where he is now revered by Hindus, Muslims, Buddhists and, of course, Christians. Later, Xavier was declared patron of all the foreign missions along with St Thérèse of Lisieux.

Despite Alexandro Valignano's grave doubts about the miracles attributed to Xavier, he does suggest that two things struck him in particular about Xavier – 'his largeness of heart … his trustful confidence in God … and the second one, which has greatly amazed me … is how he joined action and contemplation' (Quoted in Bermejo, p. 303).

Xavier's ceaseless apostolic journeying and activity are legendary. The beatification process of 1556 confirms that on the Fishery Coast, 'He never rested one month, never three weeks in the same place, making his journeys on foot and sometimes barefooted' (Quoted in Léon-Dufour, p. 186). One can only be amazed at the thousands of miles he travelled by sea, often in treacherous conditions. His ministry to all in need, temporal or spiritual, was endless – to royal court officials in Lisbon; on board ships to the passengers and crews; to the sick and the poor in hospitals and prisons wherever he went; to lepers; to the Paravas on the Fishery Coast. Yet, despite all this apostolic activity, Xavier always had time for prayer. Father Antonio de Quadros said of Xavier, 'During the day he belonged wholly to his fellowmen, at night he belonged wholly to God … he would sleep no more than three or four hours during the night … He could be seen out of doors during part of the night, eyes raised and filled with tears, before the starry sky' (Léon-Dufour, pp. 134–35). Xavier had one thing in common with Ignatius: both had the gift of tears in prayer, particularly during the celebration of the Mass. Xavier was often seen lost in prayer before his crucifix. His intense activity with people during the day impelled him to commune with God in the peaceful silence of the night.

In the midst of all his physical hardships, Xavier is reported to have kept his gaiety and cheerfulness. Father Melchior Nunes Barreto reported to Portugal, 'What affability he has, always smiling with a calm and cheerful face, always smiling but never laughing. Always smiling because he has a spiritual joy' (Schurhammer, Vol. IV, p. 501). Innumerable witnesses who knew him personally come back repeatedly to this feature of Xavier's character, 'He used to do everything with great joy … always very happy and pleasant … for he always went about with a joyful face' (Schurhammer, Vol. II, p. 224).

At Amboina, Xavier had been told of the famous Moro Islands, which were reported as being inhabited by headhunters and cannibals, treacherous people and expert poisoners. His friends tried to dissuade him from going. He brushed aside all their objections and wrote to his Jesuit companions in Europe on 10 May 1546, 'I hope to go to an island where they eat their foes … I am going there since I have placed all my trust in God (Costelloe, pp. 140–42). After his return from the Moro Islands, where he had lived in almost constant danger of death, he speaks of the 'great and continuous spiritual consolations he had experienced there' (Costelloe, p. 172).

Though much of Xavier's decade in the East was spent alone (that is, not in the company of his Jesuit companions), we can never doubt his affection for his confrères. The Society of Jesus was for him 'a Society of Love'. He always thought fondly of his first Jesuit companions at the University of Paris, wearing their signatures, along with the formula of his final vows, in a locket around his neck. He always begged for and looked forward to long newsy letters from his companions. He called Ignatius 'our blessed Father Ignatius or the saintly Father Ignatius' (Schurhammer, Vol. IV p. 521). He was particularly fond of Ignatius 'the father of my soul'. He was convinced that, after God, he owed everything to Ignatius.

Ignatius and Xavier had two different styles of government. This is clearly reflected in the kind of obedience they demanded from their respective subjects. Whereas Ignatius rarely pulls rank and demands submission 'in virtue of holy obedience', Xavier seems to be unable to command without use of this formula. In his dealings with Xavier, Ignatius uses the formula only twice: when appointing him Provincial of the East and when recalling him to Europe. Nowhere else. In his letters to Jesuits spread far and wide, Ignatius's tendency is to give instructions but then, basically, to write, 'Do what you think best in the circumstances in which you find yourself.'

In contrast, Xavier demanded exact and prompt obedience to himself. He could be hard with some Jesuits in the extreme, even ruthless, especially when dismissing people from the Society. One single failure in the area of obedience was enough for him to throw somebody out of the Society – one thinks of poor young Alvaro Ferreira. In the chapter of the Jesuit Constitutions on dismissals, Ignatius states clearly that the Superior 'should confer with one or more persons in the house who seem more suitable and hear their opinions' (n. 221). Xavier never seems to have consulted anyone about dismissals! A letter from Ignatius to Xavier, dated 5 July 1553, obviously too late, yet interesting in itself, advises Xavier that he and other superiors should appoint consultors to advise them on matters of greater moment and only then, when the superior had listened to his consultors, should he decide on these matters. Such a procedure had so obviously not been Xavier's way of governing. He decided alone.

Xavier's too-quick theological formation in Paris was very unfortunate. His theology concerning the salvation of the unbaptised was woefully inadequate. He repeatedly makes the rash statement in his correspondence that an unbaptised adult is to go to hell. We have seen how some of Xavier's confrères disagreed strongly with his method of hasty baptisms. Ignatius, too, had strong reservations about these baptisms without a preceding catechetical instruction. Unlike some of his Parisian companions, who continued some private study of theology after their ordination, according to a Jesuit in Goa, Xavier 'never studies or reads a book' (Quoted in Bermejo, p. 313).

Afterword

Given all that has been mentioned thus far in this short biography of Francis Xavier, what type of man, what type of saint was he? I like my saints to be inspiring figures but to be deeply human as well. In that way, I feel that they give us some hope of eventual salvation!

Xavier was so obviously a complex, rich personality. He was a man of deep faith and trust in the Christ he preached. This faith and trust was nourished by a constant life of prayer, often into the deep watches of the night. The example of his life of missionary zeal and courage was a source of inspiration, not only for those in the foreign lands in which he laboured, Jesuits and laity alike, but also in the universities of Europe where his letters from these then strange lands were read and caused a sensation.

As we have seen the adjectives 'joyful', 'jovial', 'cheerful', 'loving' and 'affectionate' were often applied to Xavier. We're told that he was forever smiling but never laughing! This might suggest a certain degree of self-control. He had a special place in his heart and memory for Ignatius Loyola, Pierre Favre and Simon Rodrigues, although once Xavier left Europe they would never see each other again. Though very affectionate by temperament, he appears to have been naturally reserved with his 'Jesuit subjects' in foreign lands. Self-disclosure did not come easily to him. His cheerful manner, however, seems to have made him almost, but not always, irresistible to those to whom he tried to minister.

Xavier laid great stress on feelings of 'interior consolation' when making decisions about where next to go on mission. For example, he writes to Micer Paolo, on 8 May 1545, 'With great interior consolation I have felt and have come to know that it is God's will that I go to the regions of Malacca' (Costelloe, p. 128). On another occasion, he writes to his companions in Rome of 'experiencing such great consolation' during a storm at sea (Costelloe, p. 179). In a letter to Ignatius from Cochin on 12 January 1549, Xavier tells Ignatius, 'I have with much interior satisfaction, decided to go to this land [Japan]' (Costelloe, pp. 219–23). In other words, Xavier tends to use the Second Time for Making an Election, according to the *Spiritual Exercises* [176], 'when enough light and knowledge is received by experience of consolations and desolations, and by the experience of the discernment of the various spirits'.

In a letter dated 13 January 1542, Xavier tells his companions in Rome that in the two-and-a-half years since he sailed from Portugal, he had received only one letter from them (Bermejo, p. 94). I agrec with Bermejo (p. 92) that temperamentally Xavier appears to be a paradox. On the one hand, he showed himself to be always outgoing and sociable, kind and jovial, enjoying the company of others. Yet, on the other, his life in the East is often marked by an unusual loneliness, not only because loneliness was thrust upon him, but also because he seems to have sought it deliberately. During his first stay in India, which lasted about three-and-a-half years (from early May 1542 to the end of August 1545), Xavier spent all the time alone without the company of any other Jesuit, even when he had the opportunity of living with one. In Indonesia, it will be much the same and, to a lesser extent, again later in Japan. During his two-year stay in Japan, Xavier did not receive a single letter from anybody. It was only later, when he reached Malacca, on his way back from India, that he learned of the siege of Malacca by enemy forces, which drastically cut off all possible communications with Japan.

Xavier had an innate tendency to be always on the move – he had an active, almost restive temperament – but, humanly, he must, at times, have experienced tremendous loneliness. In the extant correspondence of Xavier, there is never any mention of personal loneliness but there is a consistent imploring of the brethren in Rome to write to him and inform him of all that is happening in the Society.

Allowing for times of inevitable loneliness, Xavier is always effusive in his expressions of brotherly love for his Jesuit confrères in Rome, Lisbon and elsewhere. For Xavier, the Society of Jesus was 'a Society of Love'. He writes, 'If I should ever forget the Society of the name of Jesus may my right hand be forgotten … The debt which I owe to this Society … I am saying this in order to avoid the sin of ingratitude' (Quoted in Bermejo, p.93). His dearest wish was that his companion from Paris days, Simon Rodrigues, would join him in the East. This was never to happen.

Xavier was so obviously a man of tremendous courage – he is not daunted by the prospect of going among the headhunters on the Moro Islands; he will challenge the Japanese *bonzes* to their faces about their obvious sexual immorality; he does not shirk from reminding King John III of Portugal of his Christian duty to desist from the economic exploitation of the Indies, otherwise the king will pay for such neglect in the next life!

Bermejo is correct in his summation of Xavier's character (p. 310) as being 'an exceptional missionary but a mediocre superior'. We have seen how the Jesuit brethren in Goa wrote to Ignatius to complain about Xavier's all too frequent and prolonged absences; how such long absences made it impossible for him fully to appreciate the situation in St Paul's College. Xavier was a restless character, always in a hurry to be off to the next mission field. He was a maverick.

Xavier had a black-and-white attitude with regard to Jesuit obedience. He judged the slightest suspicion of a breach in obedience *to him* as showing a lack of humility in the Jesuit subject and as meriting instant dismissal from the Society. He was much too harsh in this regard, not allowing for consultation with other Jesuits. Xavier decided and that was it!

Thank God Xavier was human, after all – there is some hope for the rest of us!

Ironically, as I am bringing this short biography to a close, a Jesuit confrère has brought to my attention that Pope Francis spoke recently about Xavier at a General Audience (17 May 2023). Francis mentions Xavier's apostolic zeal, which enabled him to go 'to the frontiers'. He describes Xavier as *il grande sognatore* – 'the great dreamer' – hence, the title of this book. The Pope says that it was the love of and for Christ that drove Xavier to the furthest reaches of the world; that enabled him to overcome failure and discouragement and gave him joy and consolation in following and serving Christ to the end. Pope Francis speaks of Xavier's intense missionary activity being united to his prayer life – prayer was his strength.

We can pray to St Francis Xavier, asking him to intercede for us with the Christ he served so generously and announced so bravely to the nations of the East.

Novena of Grace

Every year throughout the world there is held immediately before 12 March, the date of Xavier's canonisation, a solemn novena in his honour called the Novena of Grace. The annual nine days of public veneration and intercession seems to have originated from a great and perfectly attested miracle worked by Xavier on 3 January 1634 – the instantaneous cure of Father Marcello Mastrilli, subsequently a martyr of Japan, who lay at death's door from a grave lesion of the brain. There were several eyewitnesses to the event, including the future Jesuit Superior-General, Father Vincent Caraffa (1585–1649). This Novena of Grace is very well attended by the faithful to this day in churches throughout the Roman Catholic countries of the world.

This is the St Francis Xavier Novena Prayer:

O most kind and loving saint, in union with you I adore the Divine Majesty. The remembrance of the favours with which God blessed you during life, and of your glory after death, fills me with joy; and I unite with you in offering to God my humble tribute of thanksgiving and of praise.

I implore of you to secure for me, through your powerful intercession, the all-important blessing of living and dying in the state of grace. I also beseech you to obtain for me the favour I ask in this Novena (here mention the favour to be asked for); but if what I ask is not for the glory of God or for the good of my soul, obtain for me what is most conducive to both. Amen.

Select Bibliography

Abbott, Walter M., SJ (ed.), *The Documents of Vatican II*, London: Geoffrey Chapman, 1966.

Bermejo, Luis M., SJ, *Unto the Indies – Life of St. Francis Xavier*, Anand, Gujarat: Gujarat Sahita Prakash, 2000.

Brodrick, James, SJ, *The Origin of the Jesuits*, London, New York, Toronto: Longmans, Green and Co., 1940.

— *The Progress of the Jesuits*, London, New York, Toronto: Longmans, Green and Co., 1946.

— *St Francis Xavier*, London: Burns & Oates, 1952.

Costelloe, M. Joseph, SJ (trans.), *The Letters and Instructions of Francis Xavier, translated and introduced by M. Joseph SJ*, St Louis, MO: The Institute of Jesuit Sources, 1992.

De Guibert, Joseph, SJ, *The Jesuits: Their Spiritual Doctrine and Practice – A Historical Study*, St Louis, MO: The Institute of Jesuit Sources, in cooperation with Loyola University Press, Chicago, 1964.

Léon-Dufour, Xavier, SJ, *St. Francis Xavier – The Mystical Progress of the Apostle* (trans. Henry Pascual Oiz SJ), Bombay: St Paul Publications, 1976.

O'Malley, John, SJ, *The First Jesuits*, Cambridge, MA: Harvard University Press, 1993.

Schurhammer, Georg, SJ, *Francis Xavier – His Life, His Times* (trans. M. Joseph Costelloe SJ), Rome: The Jesuit Historical Institute, 1973–82.

Worcester, Thomas, SJ, (ed.), *The Cambridge Companion to the Jesuits*, Cambridge: Cambridge University Press, 2008.